Becoming Whole

Letters To The Woman I Am

LORNA OWENS

All rights reserved.

No part of this publication may be reproduced, stored in a retrieval system, or transmitted in any form or by any means—electronic, mechanical, photocopying, recording, or otherwise—without prior written permission from the publisher, except for brief quotations used in reviews or scholarly works.

First Edition: 2025 Printed in the United States of America

ISBN: 978-0-9790778-2-1

Cover Design: Desert Sage Lifestyle
Interior Layout and Design: Lorna Owens
Publisher: Desert Sage Lifestyle Wellness
Website: www.desert-sage.co

This book is a work of reflection and inspiration. It is not intended as medical or legal advice.

For rights, permissions, or wholesale inquiries, please contact:
Desert Sage Lifestyle Wellness
101 Artisan Alley
DeLand, Florida, USA
Email: sales@desert-sage.co

Desert Sage Lifestyle supports education for women tea farmers and midwives around the world. Your purchase helps fund this mission.

Lorna Owens Esq
305-505-5493
www.desert-Sage.co
www.footprints-foundation.org

Also By Lorna Owens

Desert Sage Wonderful World of Tea: From Ancient Leaves to Modern Wellness

Everyday Grace Everyday Miracle Living the Life You were Born to Live.

My Journey with Food During the Time of Coronavirus.

Dedication

To all the women who have loved and lost—

and still chose to rise. Even when worry wrapped
itself around your ribcage, even when you couldn't
sleep for the weight of it, you rose.

To the women who whispered prayers through tears,
who showed up anyway, who gave love another chance.

To those now held in the arms of mad, beautiful,
radical love this is for you.

To my sister Veronica, whose steady soul softens my worry.
To Maxine, whose sense of humor pushes the clouds away.
To my brother Wayne, your strength has been my shield.
To my sister-in-law Yvonne, thank you for your kindness.

I love you all more than you know.

You remind me that I am not alone.
May we all continue becoming.
Even when we worry.
Even when we wonder.
We are still worthy.
We are still whole.

Lorna

Prologue

Born of Love

This book was born when I loved—not carefully,
not timidly, but with the full fire of my heart.
It was born in the quiet moments
when I gave of myself freely, when I stood bare,
open, unguarded.
And then I loved abandonedly.
With trembling hands and a fearless soul,
I gave love a place to rest in me.
And in return, I tasted its sweetness.

I have known what it means to be held.
And I have known the hollow silence
of being left behind.
I have laughed with my whole body.
And I have wept in the stillness of my room
when no one was watching.
But it was in the loving,
in the letting go,
in the holding on,
in the breaking open,
and the rising again that I found myself.
Not the version the world applauded.
Not the polished, performing version.
But the one who waited patiently
for my own return.

Whole.
Unapologetic.
Radiant in her truth.

These letters are not just memories.
They are markers—
breadcrumbs on the path
of my becoming.
They tell the story of a woman
who dared to love
and survived it.
A woman who learned that loss is not the end.
It is often the beginning.
So, I offer these pages to you, dear reader,
dear sister, dear seeker.
May they remind you
that love, even when it shatters,
can shape you into someone more whole
than you ever imagined.

Love,

Lorna

Contents

Dedication ii

Prologue iii

The Day I Chose to Return to Myself 1

I Was Here to Love You 5

I Make No Apology for Loving Hard 9

Sit and I Sip Tea 11

I Sit in My Chair: 13

A Space for Love Worthy of Me 13

My Silence Is Wisdom 16

The Wake-Up Call 19

You Don't Send Me Roses 22

When Love Knocks, Gently 25

You Didn't Fight for Me 28

To My Readers of Becoming Whole 31

Reflection Prompt: Knowing Your Worth 33

Are You Missing Me? 34

Thank You for Loving Me 37

The Beauty of Boundaries 41

Away Without Closure 44

Why I Hesitate 47

Sit With Tea and Truth 50

Could You Love This Woman? 53

Choose You 57

I See Your Grief, ... 63

Even When You Don't Speak It 63

A Man of Substance 69

To the One I Loved: A Prayer from My Chair 73

I Claim Elegance and Quiet Things 76

Space between the Thought 79

A Good Reckoning 84

I Come from a Line of Strong Women 87

I Sit in My Favorite Chair: The Company I Keep 89

I Am the Prayer of My Ancestors 91

Let the Soft Life Find You 93

Letter to Myself: I Finally Got It 95

Wanted A Man Who Can Handle A Woman Who Knows Her Power 98

When Destiny Called My Name 100

Letter to Self – Sweet Surrender 104

Never Ever Settle 108

Walk Away 111

The Waiting 114

The Woman of Worth 117

I Sit in My Favorite Chair 121

Food as Soul Ceremony 124

Dream a Bigger Dream 127

Love Finds Me in My Cup 131

Letter to Myself: The Wind Carries Me 133

Letter to Myself: Loving Is Worth It. 137

Grateful for the Becoming 140

I Have a Purpose 144

I Lay That Burden Down 147

Today, I Feel Divine 150

The Third Act 152

A Letter to My Future Self 155

Circle of Women 159

The Story Is Mine to Tell 162

Letter to My Sisters – The Invitation to Rise 165

The Valley and the Mountaintop 168

You Are Stronger Than You Know 171

The Woman Who Thrives 174

How Do You Like Me Now? 177

I Am a Healer 182

Reclaim 185

My Why 187

I Carry the Wisdom of All the Women 190

 Before Me 190

I'm Sorry for All the Times I Didn't Choose You 192

I Sit Sipping My Tea, Dancing in the Light 194

You Are Not Behind—You Are Becoming 196

The Woman I Saw in My Reflection 201

And So, I Rise 204

Today I Sit in My Chair with English Breakfast 208

Today I Sit in My Chair with Determination 211

and Tea 211

The Mirror Doesn't Lie. 215

The Most Important Decision 220

Letter to Self – Choose Your Peace. 225

What It Means to Become Whole. 227

Embracing Self-Acceptance and Growth 228

A Journey into Self-Acceptance and Growth 230

How to Become a Woman 239

Ritual Matters 244

Dear Heart – A Letter on Healing 247

Morning Reverie: A Letter to the Woman I Am 250

Becoming Woman: The Quiet Arrival 254

Losing Ceremony – Welcome Home to Yourself 257

Letters To The Woman I Am Collection 264

LETTER ONE

The Day I Chose to Return to Myself

Dear Woman I Am,

I sit in my chair—
the one that holds my weary and my wonder.
I wrap my hands around a cup of tea
and the steam curls upward like a quiet prayer.
A hush settles over me, the kind of stillness
that only comes when you stop performing
and start remembering.
There is something sacred in this ritual.

In this tea.
In this moment.
It is not just a pause.
It is a coming home.
I think back to the day I returned to myself.
Not a grand moment.
Not a loud revelation.
But a quiet reckoning.
A mirror.
A pair of tired eyes staring back at me—
eyes that looked familiar,
but not quite mine.
She wore my face.

She carried my memories.
She held the weight of every sacrifice—the silent ones,
the celebrated ones, and the ones that nearly broke me.
But her eyes.
They were not searching for applause.
They were not chasing perfection.
They were looking for something deeper.
They were looking for me.
That was the day I laid it all down.
The titles.
The roles.
The masks I wore so well.
I was not the attorney.
Not the midwife.
Not the fixer, the achiever,
the author, the international speaker.
I was not the one who always knew what to say.
I was the woman underneath it all—soft, aching, and holy.
The one who once loved with open hands.
The one who believed love could be a sanctuary.
The one who lost pieces of herself along the way,
but still whispered, Come back home.

This book was born in that return.
It was born in the raw tenderness of love—
the kind of love that gives without condition,
that leaps without certainty,
that surrenders without a backup plan.
It was born in the sacred ache of loss—
of giving and grieving,

of holding and letting go,
of breaking open and rising again.
Because I have loved.
And I have lost.
And I have learned that heartbreak does not mean you failed—
it means you felt. It means you lived.
And somewhere in the rubble,
I met myself again.
Not the polished version.
Not the woman who makes everything look easy.
But the woman who cries during old songs.
The one who still believes in magic.
The one who was broken—
and still chose to love again.

So, I write this letter not to mourn what left,
but to honor what stayed.
What was found.
What was reborn.
To you, the woman I am:
Your softness is not a flaw.
It is your strength.
Your vulnerability is not your weakness.
It is your brilliance.
Your love—yes, even the love that was not returned—was holy.
It was a doorway. It brought you back to yourself.
So, keep choosing yourself.
Keep drinking your tea.
Keep listening to the whispers inside.
Keep becoming whole.

You are not behind.
You are not too late.
You are already returning

Love, always,

Lorna

LETTER TWO

I Was Here to Love You

I sit again, in my chair.
My cup is warm—
a soft lavender Earl Grey today.
It wraps itself around me like memory.
And I sip slowly, because this letter comes not from anger,
but from love.

I want you to know:
I was here to love you.
Not to hurt you.
Not to tame you.
Not to mold you into anything other
than the man you already were becoming.

Your freedom was never in danger with me.
I only ever stood at the edge of your wings,
cheering as you stretched them,
as you flew.

My soul broke open the day I saw you laughing—
truly laughing—with your head tilted back and your spirit
momentarily unburdened.
My soul broke open
when you traveled far and wide,

chasing what made you feel alive.
And still, I did not try to hold you back.

I did not come to possess.
I came to witness.
To stand in quiet reverence
for the man who had forgotten
what tenderness could be.

I do not know why it was so hard for you—
maybe before your grief
settled into your bones like fog,
love had already become complicated.
Perhaps romance had grown dim
and trust was something buried deep
beneath years of self-reliance and silent ache.

You turned inward.
You pulled only what served you.
Only what gave you lightness.
But in doing so,
you locked so many doors—even the ones I knocked on with
gentle hands and open heart.
I was not there to knock them down.
I only ever wanted to sit beside you,
to speak to you tenderly in private,
and honor you with my presence in public.
To never dim your light.
To always walk beside your greatness,
never in competition with it.

I would have held you in grace.
Spoken your name with reverence.
Protected your silences.
Celebrated your joy.

But love is not a solo act.
And trust is not a one-way street.

You must learn to let go.
You must learn to receive as much as you give.

You must believe that to love deeply
is not to lose yourself—but to find more
of who you are in the eyes of someone
who sees you completely.

So, I ask you, gently—not out of desperation,
but from a place of final clarity:
Look me in the eyes.
Tell me, truly—do you feel nothing?
Nothing for me?

If that is your truth, then let it be so.
Let silence be our final blessing.
Let honesty be the way we part.

But know this—I was here to love you.
And I did.
Softly.

Boldly.
Unapologetically.

And even as I sip this last bit of tea,
I leave nothing bitter behind.
Only truth.
Only love.
Only the knowing that I showed up with all of me
and that I loved you the best way I knew how.

Love,

Lorna

LETTER THREE

I Make No Apology for Loving Hard

I sip tea.
I sit in my chair. You wonder why?
Because this is sacred sanctuary to me—
a holy place where my heart can exhale,
where my soul is allowed to feel without apology.
And while I sit here, I will tell you something
you might not know about me:
I love hard. I care deeply. I do not know how to love halfway.
If you are my friend, you are written into my prayers,
woven into the fabric of my daily thoughts.
I will remember what makes you smile,
what burdens your spirit,
what kind of tea soothes your sorrow.
I will go the extra mile—without hesitation,
without conditions.
Because that is the rhythm of my heart.
Because friendship, to me, is not surface.
It is sacred. It is deep like ancestral wells,
rich like the soil of the motherland,
unshaken by storms.
I have been told I feel too much.
That I wear my heart too loud.
But I will not mute it.
I make no apology for caring deeply,

for loving wildly, for showing up when others fade.
It is not weakness—it is my power.
Some hearts are built for boundaries.
Mine is built for bridges
And if you ever wondered why I light candles for those I love,
why I remember the small things,
why I cry when others are hurting,
why I give even when I'm empty—
it is because I know the world needs more tenderness,
not less.
So no, I won't apologize for being too much.
Too kind. Too loyal. Too loving. Too soft.
Because there is nothing too much
about showing up with your whole heart.
And I will continue to sit in this chair,
to sip my tea,
to pour love like it's water from a sacred spring.
Because that is who I am.
And that is enough.

Love,

Lorna

LETTER FOUR

Sit and I Sip Tea

I sit and I sip tea in my favorite chair.
It is warm.
It is inviting.
It is the place where the world quiets,
and I remember who I am.

The steam rises like a prayer,
and in that sacred curl of heat and silence,
I find my solace.
I find my strength.
This is my sanctuary not because it hides me,
but because it reveals me.

In the hush of this moment,
I am reminded of my responsibility
not only to myself, but to those who will come after me.

Especially the young women.
Those just finding their voice,
those learning to walk in shoes that do not yet fit,
those daring to dream beyond the borders they were given.
I must drop seeds of hope in their path—
not randomly,
but intentionally.

Seeds of courage.
Seeds of resilience.
Seeds of belonging.

It is not enough to plant them.
I must nourish them.
Water them with my wisdom.
Shield them from the winds of doubt.
Teach them to stand tall, even in storms.

And just as importantly,
I must make sure they see the seeds.
That they recognize the garden beneath their feet.
That they know someone came before them
and thought of them.
Loved them.
Believed in them.

And I must teach them,
in quiet conversation and bold example,
to do the same—to scatter their own seeds
for the daughters of tomorrow.
So, the chain never breaks.
So, the light never dims.
So, the world always remembers
the power of a woman who sits,
who sips, and who dares to sow hope into the future.
Love as Always,

Lorna

LETTER FIVE

I Sit in My Chair:

A Space for Love Worthy of Me

I sit with my tea in my usual chair.
Steam curls like prayers rising gentle, warm, sure.
And I breathe into the quiet knowing that fills my chest.
This much I know:
I want to be chosen, not simply picked.

Picked is random.
Picked is convenient.
Picked is standing on a shelf,
waiting to be noticed by someone
who isn't even sure what they're looking for.

But chosen.
Chosen is sacred.
Chosen is deliberate.
Chosen is seeing my soul and saying, "Yes, her."
Not because I'm perfect.
But because I'm real, and enough,
and whole in all my becoming.
So, until such time,
I leave space.
Sacred space.
For the one who comes not to fill a void,

but to build a home beside me.
He will see me not just the light in my eyes when I smile,
but the shadows I carry quietly.
He will treat me with intention,
with care in the small things,
with kindness in the pauses,
with reverence in the chaos.

There is one.
Yes, one.
who is loving, not just in grand gestures,
but in everyday offerings:
The soft check-in when the world overwhelms.
The joy that bubbles when my smile breaks through.
The hand on my back when I don't ask for it,
but need it just the same.
He won't ask me to shrink.
He won't silence my strength.
He will dance with my dreams
and sit in stillness with my sorrow.
He will choose me freely, fiercely, daily.
Not someone who fits me in between the lines of his schedule,
but one who writes me into the rhythm of his days.

So, I sip my tea.
And I wait not passively, but with dignity, with peace.
Because I know what I deserve.
And I know love like that is possible.

And I am already enough.

Whether he comes tomorrow
or not at all.
I am already enough.
But still,
I leave the light on.

Until Then,

Lorna

LETTER SIX

My Silence Is Wisdom

My tea beckons me.
My chair beckons me.
And I respond—early in the hush of morning,
before the world begins its noise.
I sit.
I sip.
And I allow the stillness to speak.
My silence is not emptiness.
It is not retreat.
It is not absence.
My silence is wisdom.
When I sit quietly in your presence,
or in the presence of others, it is not because
I have nothing to say,
nothing to offer,
nothing to contribute.
It is because I have learned—
through love, through loss, through living
that sometimes silence holds more truth than words.
I have learned that stillness is power.
That a woman can know deeply, feel fully,
and still choose not to fill the space.
Sometimes, silence is my strength.
Sometimes, silence is my sanctuary.

Sometimes, silence is the only safe language I have left.
And yet I wonder...
Do you notice me when I am quiet?
Do you notice that I'm not engaged?
Do you sense the shifting in my spirit?
Do you wonder why? Do you lean-in, curious, gentle?
Do you ask without demanding,
listen without interrupting?

Do you consider whether I am not feeling well?
Whether something beneath the surface has unsettled me?
Do you consider that perhaps I am uncomfortable navigating
a room, a conversation, a moment that does not make space
for me? And if you do...
Would you reach for me?
Would you say something tender to make me feel like I belong?
Would you offer a glance that says, I see you. I've got you.
Would you hold my hand—
maybe not in public,
but in presence—
so that I feel safe enough to exhale?

Or would you let me sit there, fending for myself
in a world that too often forgets the quiet women
the sensitive souls,
the ones who feel everything but say very little?
You see, my silence is not your cue to dismiss me.
It is your invitation to notice me more deeply.

Because silence, for me, is sacred.

It is the way I listen to my heart.
It is the way I honor my boundaries.
It is the way I survive.
And so, I sit. I sip.
And I wait for the one who understands that even in silence,

I am still speaking.

With love and stillness,

Lorna

LETTER SEVEN

The Wake-Up Call

This morning,
I sit again—tea in hand,
cradled by the arms of my old faithful chair.

The steam rises slowly,
but there is no softness in this cup today.
This is not the kind of tea that soothes.
This is the kind that awakens.

This is the moment I stop pretending.
The moment I stop romanticizing my own unraveling,
my own ache, my own demise.

Healing is not poetic.
It is not neatly wrapped in scented candles and reggae music.
Healing is brutal.
It will tear the illusion from your hands
and ask you to sit in the truth you've tried to sweeten.

And the truth?
Some of what I called love
was only loneliness dressed in hope.

Some of the people I clung to

were never meant to stay.
They were never meant to even enter—
but I left the door wide open
and called it destiny.

I dragged them into chapters
they had no business reading.
I assigned them roles in stories
they were never meant to act in.

And now—this is the wake-up call.
The part where I stop making excuses
for those who offered me pieces
when I came with my whole.

The part where I say:
Leave.
Let go.
Release what was never rooted.

Stop weaving tragedy into romance.
Stop calling chaos chemistry.
Stop mistaking temporary comfort
for soul connection.

Because truth lives here now.
And I want what is real.
Even if it hurts.
Even if it strips me bare.

So, no more illusions.
No more softness where fire is needed.
No more dressing wounds with pretty words.
Let it burn.
Let it bruise.
Let it break.

Because this is how the healing begins—
not in denial, but in reckoning.

And I will not be afraid to look at what hurt me and say:
You no longer belong here.

I exit now.
Quietly.
Clearly.
Completely.

And I leave them behind—
the ones who were never meant to stay,

the ones I chose before I chose myself.
Today, I walk toward wholeness.
And this time, I do not look back.

Love,

Lorna

LETTER EIGHT

You Don't Send Me Roses

Good morning, world.
I sit here for a moment— tea in hand, in my favorite chair,
before the rush,
before the world fully exhales
and stretches into its noise.
The light is soft.
The quiet is kind.
And in this tender space between breath and becoming,
a thought tiptoes in—
You don't send me roses.
And I wonder why. I wonder if you know
how deeply I cherish beauty.
How a single bloom can make me pause—
how petals feel like poetry,
how fragrance can summon memory,
how the softness of a rose
mirrors the way I love.
You don't send me roses.
Not because I ask,
but because you don't think to.
Or perhaps you never learned

that some women bloom

when they are chosen with intention.

Not for the grand gesture,

but for the knowing.

I am the woman who notices small things.

The one who brews tea with care,

who lights candles just because,

who leaves notes in margins,

and speaks in gestures that whisper,

You matter to me.

And maybe, just maybe, I want to be met with that same sacred softness.

Not because I need a bouquet to feel loved,

but because it would say, I see you. I thought of you today.

You deserve beauty too.

You don't send me roses.

And it's not just about the flowers.

It's about thoughtfulness.

About paying attention.

About being known in the quiet places

where I rarely speak my longings out loud.

Still... I sit.

Still… I sip.
And still… I bloom.
Because even if no roses arrive,
I remain a garden—
wild and worthy.
Soft and sure.
Rooted in love that does not beg,
only hopes to be met.

With tea, tenderness,

Lorna

LETTER NINE

When Love Knocks, Gently

I sit in my chair.
And I sip tea.
A quiet green tea today—earthy, alive, honest.
The kind of tea that doesn't ask for attention
but lingers in your senses anyway.

And I wonder.
Do you know what you want from love now,
at this time of your life?
Do you trust the trembling of your own heart?
Or have you built a fortress,
stone by stone, to keep even the warmest light out?

Because I see it—you are cautious now.
Measured.
Holding yourself like fragile china
too many hands mishandled.
But Beloved,
what if this love—this gentle, clear-eyed love—
is not here to break you?
What if love is knocking now,
not with fanfare, but with barefoot sincerity?

You say the timing is off.

You say you are not ready.
You say you're still finding your breath
after all those almosts and never agains.

But let me say this—

Real love does not demand readiness.
It asks only for presence.
It arrives like dawn—quiet, certain,
whether or not you are awake to receive it.

So, if it comes—with kindness in its voice,
with stillness in its hands,
with respect in its rhythm—
don't rush to close the door.
Don't analyze the angles.
Don't measure your preparedness like a checklist.
Just listen.
And if something in your spirit softens,
if something in your chest opens
without warning,
let it.

Let it.

Because love like this, my kind of love—
the one that sees soul before skin,
laughter before logic, and truth before timing—
it doesn't come often.
So, even if it arrives when your hair is still wet from grief,

when your house is still messy with healing,
when your heart still stammers at the thought of vulnerability—
Choose it.
Choose love.

Not because it is perfect.
But because it is real.
And it came anyway.

With all tenderness,

Lorna

LETTER TEN

You Didn't Fight for Me

I sit in my chair.
Today, I drink a beautiful tea from Assam—dark, malty,
full-bodied.
It tastes like truth.
Strong and steady, like the women who harvest it at dawn
in the monsoon-washed fields of northeastern India.
Assam tea is not delicate.
It does not whisper.
It announces itself with presence,
with depth—the kind of tea that stays long after the sip is gone.

And as I sip,
I think of us.
Of how we ended.
Of the words I said—yes, I said them.

I told you I didn't like how you were treating me.
I told you I didn't feel respected.
I told you that maybe, just maybe,
it was best for us to go our own way.

And you agreed.
We agreed.
And I meant it.

I meant every syllable
spoken through clenched strength and quiet resolve.
But then…
I didn't.
Not really.
I thought—no, I hoped—you would soften.

That you would feel my absence
and come back with tenderness.
That you would show up,
call, stand in front of me and say,
"Let's talk. Let's try."
Because I believed—when love is real,

you fight for it.
Even when it's hard.
Even when it's messy.
Even when your pride is bruised
and your comfort is disrupted.
I believed that if you love someone,
really love them, you fight.
You reach for them, even when their words sting.
You walk into the storm
because they are worth the weathering it for.

But you didn't fight for me.

You didn't come.
You didn't call.
You took it all personally—my pain, my honesty, my fear.

You saw an attack,
when all I wanted was connection.
You saw rejection,
when all I offered was truth.

You didn't see that I was hurting.
You didn't see that I loved you.
That I was doing the best I could
while trying to hold myself together.

You didn't see me.

And maybe that is the final ache—
not that we ended,
but that you didn't even try.
Still, I sit in my chair.
Still, I sip my Assam.
And still, I choose to heal.

Because even though you didn't fight for me,
I will always fight for myself.
With a soft, steady heart,

Lorna

LETTER ELEVEN

To My Readers of Becoming Whole

Dear Beautiful Soul,

Today, I sit in my favorite chair, tea warm in my hands, and I feel the fullness of this truth settling into my spirit. Becoming whole means that I know my worth. It means that I have stopped discounting myself. I have stopped twisting myself into a shape that is unrecognizable just to fit into someone else's life. The price of access to me is simple: honor me. Treat me as I deserve to be treated. Listen when I speak. Show up in love and kindness. Respect my heart, my time, my energy, and my spirit. That is all.

If he cannot do that—if he cannot meet you with love, grace, and the smallest gestures of consideration—then you release him without hesitation, without bitterness. Move on with your life, radiant and whole. Pour every ounce of that love you were so willing to give into yourself. Build your dreams. Walk in purpose. Adorn your life with laughter, joy, travel, books, music, and friendship.

Never, ever let anyone take you for granted. You are not a consolation prize. You are not "lucky" to be chosen. You are the gift. You are the wonder. You are the miracle someone prays for and then pinches themselves when they meet.

So, my sister, never sell yourself short. Never dim your light for someone unwilling to rise to meet your brilliance. and you are wonderfully made. With all my love and all my courage,

Lorna

LETTER TWELVE

Reflection Prompt: Knowing Your Worth

Take a quiet moment with your journal. Pour yourself a cup of your favorite tea, breathe deeply, and write from your heart:

1. Where in my life have I accepted less than I deserve?
2. What does being treated with love and respect look like for me?
3. If I fully honored my worth, what would I stop tolerating?
4. What beautiful things will I focus my energy on when I choose myself first?

End your reflection with this affirmation, written three times in your journal:

I am beautiful, sacred, and wonderfully made. I will never settle for less than I deserve.

Lorna

LETTER THIRTEEN

Are You Missing Me?

I sit in my chair.
And I sip my tea—
English Breakfast, bold, familiar,
the kind that reminds me of Sunday mornings
and things I wish I could say out loud.
It fills my chest with warmth
and my thoughts with you.

And I wonder…
Are you missing me?

When you were alone last night,
did your thoughts drift toward mine?
Did the silence of your room
make space for my name?
Did you reach for your phone
and then pull your hand back,
pretending you didn't ache?

Because I did.

I missed you.
And the ache was real.
It pulsed quietly,

a steady reminder
that something once lived here
between us.

I wonder,
do you feel it too—
that flicker of memory,
that phantom touch,
that echo of laughter
that no one else can mimic?

Are you lonely,
truly lonely,
when you're home alone with no one—
no one special?
No love to curl beside you,
no voice to ask if you're okay,
no arms to pull you close,
no one to see you fully
and still stay.

Is this all you want for your life—
the silence,
the safe distance,
the detachment disguised as peace?

Or will you let love in?

Will you allow it to cross your threshold
without shame,

without defense,
without conditions?

Because love,
real love,
requires more than a heartbeat.
It asks for courage.

And here's the question I carry
with every sip of this dark, anchoring tea:

Are you missing me?
Did you ever?

Have you had second thoughts—
not just about what was,
but about what could have been
if we had both stayed soft,
both chosen love,
both dared to fight for something rare?
I'll never know.

But tonight,
I sit here.
With tea and longing.
And I wonder.

With quiet hope,

Lorna

LETTER FOURTEEN

Thank You for Loving Me

Today, I sit in my favorite chair.
The one that holds me like memory, like prayer.
And in my cup is a deep, velvety Assam—
a black tea from India, bold and malty,
a tea that lingers like a good kiss,
like a story that refuses to be forgotten.
I sip slowly.
I sip with gratitude.
Because today,
I want to thank you.

Thank you for having loved me—
or maybe it was like, or lust, or the warm intoxication
of two spirits dancing near flame.
But whatever it was,
you brought light into my life.

I was drawn to your wit,
your sophistication,
your worldly grace and cosmopolitan charm.
I admired the way you moved through the world—
elegant, decisive,
like someone who knew his place in it.
We shared deep conversations,

sharp banter,
gorgeous dinners filled with laughter and wine.
And through it all,
you brought a richness and fullness to my world
that I hadn't felt in a long, long time.
And I am grateful.

If ever there is something I can do for you—
some way I can offer you back even a flicker
of what you awakened in me—
please know I will.

Because you opened up a part of me
that had been sleeping.
A part that now knows desire,
and joy,
and the magic of being seen.

So yes, it hurt when we said goodbye.
It tore me apart in places
I didn't know could split.
It was the kind of pain that steals breath,
leaves you weeping quietly in the night,
wondering if you'll ever stop reaching
for a ghost.

I tried—oh, how I tried—to forget.
To tuck you away in a memory drawer
and walk forward untouched.

But that's not how real things work.

You touched me.
And I thank you.

Because what you gave me,
even for a season,
has prepared me for the love that is coming.

And I know it's coming.

The kind of love that lingers and builds,
the kind of love that wraps itself around me gently
and says, "I'm staying."

I am ready.

So today, with my hands wrapped around this cup,
with my heart soft and open,
I thank you.

May you find love too—
the kind that mirrors your depth,
your quiet ache,
your potential to be cherished.

I wish you joy.
I wish you peace.
And I send you off with love.

Much love.

Hugs,

Lorna

LETTER FIFTEEN

The Beauty of Boundaries

Today, I sip a simple green tea
from the foothills of the Kilimanjaro Mountains.
It is soft, grassy, and grounding—
like the truth that rises in me.

I sit in my chair,
the one that has held me through every season,
and this much I know to be true:
Boundaries are beautiful.
They are not walls.
They are windows.
They are invitations to come close—
but with care.

A boundary says:
This is who I am.
This is what I honor.
This is what I expect.
This is what I protect.

Not out of fear.
Not out of pain.
But out of love for myself.
Out of clarity.

Out of sacred knowing.

When I set a boundary, I am not pushing you away—
I am welcoming you in,
but only as your best self.
The self that listens.
The self that respects.
The self that understands
that love is not permission to disregard my peace.

Boundaries do not mean I am cold.
They mean I am clear.
They do not mean I am hard.
They mean I am whole.

When I name what I need,
when I define what I will give,
when I make space for truth—
I am not being too much.
I am being just enough
for a life that honors me.

Let there be no confusion.
Let there be no guessing games.
I will not suffer in silence
and call it love.

I will not shrink
just to make someone else comfortable.

I set boundaries because I trust myself.
I set boundaries because I am secure.
I set boundaries because I deserve to feel safe
in every room I enter
and every relationship I nourish.

This is not resistance.
This is reverence.
This is not separation.
This is sacred alignment.

And anyone who is meant to walk with me
will walk with respect.
Will walk with care.
Will walk with love—
not in spite of my boundaries,
but because of them.

So I sip my tea.
Simple. Clean. True.
And I give thanks
for the voice that rises in me
and the strength to say—

This is what I need.
This is what I offer.
And this is where I stand.

Lorna

LETTER SIXTEEN

Away Without Closure

I sit here again—
tea in hand, in my sacred chair.
The same chair that has held me
in laughter, in longing, in loss.
And today,
it holds me steady
as I speak truth to power.

Stop asking for closure.
Stop waiting for closure.
Stop begging the air, the phone, the silence
to give you what he never will.

He is not coming back with kind words.
He is not sitting somewhere with remorse.
He is not crafting a letter or planning a conversation
to ease your ache,
to offer you peace.
Because he does not see you.

He never really did.

You were a chapter, he skimmed through—
a paragraph he never fully read.

You were full color in a world
he only viewed in grayscale.
And as much as you hoped he'd find depth,
he only knew how to wade in shallow water.

So now, here you are,
soul twisted in knots,
mind spinning like an addict
searching for the next fix—
but your drug is closure.
You want a reason.
An apology.
An explanation.
You want him to understand your heart
the way you tried to understand his.

But closure will not come.
Because he has no space for you in his life.
And he's not going to make space.

And that doesn't mean you are not worthy.
It means he is not capable.
It means his love was limited
and your love was overflowing.

So, walk away.
Walk away not because you're weak,
but because you're finally strong enough
to stop waiting at a locked door.
You've knocked long enough.

And now, it's time
to find a new path—
one lined with wildflowers,
with healing,
with love that doesn't require you to shrink,
beg, or ache.

Make tea.
Take a deep breath.
And let your own silence be the closure.
Because peace is not something he can give you.
It is something you reclaim.

You don't need his goodbye.
You just need your own release.

So, walk away, love.
Not broken.
But free.

With grace,

Lorna

LETTER SEVENTEEN

Why I Hesitate

I sit again in my chair,
tea warm between my palms.
Today, the brew is deep and floral—
a golden infusion of courage and truth.
And I ask myself softly:
Why do I hesitate?

It's not because I don't feel.
It's not because I am afraid of love.
It's because I know what it costs to open.
To unfold.
To lay my heart bare in trembling hands
and hope it will be held gently.
I wouldn't unravel you.
I wouldn't pull at your seams just to watch you fall apart.
You could be vulnerable with me.
Speak slowly—
I wouldn't interrupt.
I would listen with reverence.
Because your soul deserves that kind of silence.
I would match you,
not to compete,
but to meet.
Wit for wit.

Mind for mind.
Vision for vision.
We would speak of more than survival.
We would speak of life—
of books and politics,
of music and memory,
of travels and dreams.

I know what a good man is.
He leads,
but never dominates.
He protects,
but never possesses.

A woman—
especially a woman of substance—
struggles when she does not feel safe.
She dims herself not out of weakness,
but out of weariness.

So be kind to her.
Be gentle with her.
She is not afraid to rise,
but she is tired of shrinking.

A woman of substance does not want to feel invisible.
She wants to be seen—
not just for her beauty,
but for her brilliance.
She wants to be known—

not just for how she makes you feel,
but for how she thinks,
for how she moves through the world with purpose.

That woman wants to build with you.
To share thoughts over tea.
To explore the world beside you—
not behind you.
To light your fire and keep her own lit, too.

That kind of woman will not hesitate
when she feels safe.
When she feels honored.
When she feels home.
And that woman…
is me.

Lorna

LETTER EIGHTEEN

Sit With Tea and Truth

I sit in my favorite chair, as I do.
The steam rises from my cup like a soft exhale
of all I've held in too long.
Today, it's a deep, grounding oolong.
Earthy. Real. Honest.
Much like the conversation I'm finally having with myself…
about you.

What I hate most is the ambiguity
this cruel tenderness we've fallen into,
this half-light you keep me in.
You draw me near with warmth, then disappear like mist.
I never quite know if you're arriving… or leaving.

There are days when your silence feels like absence.
And days when your presence feels like promise.
But never do I feel like I have all of you.
Not the way I give all of me to you.

I understand.
I do.
You're living with grief
a thick, relentless grief that clings to your shoulders,
that clouds your heart and dims your voice.

I know you've lost something sacred.
I know your soul is sorting through fragments.

But somewhere in that swirling storm,
you reached out and pulled me in.
And now I'm lost too
not in your grief, but in your indecision.
And that is its own kind of sorrow.

You see, I think I'm special.
Not perfect, but present.
I've been soft when the world has been sharp.
I've stood by when others would've run.
I've loved you in ways that made me tremble.
I have believed in you.

And because of that,
I believe I deserve to be held sacred.
To be protected
not just from your shadows,
but from the company of those who dim me.
You see, grief does not give permission for neglect.
And love should never be buried under the weight
of what once was.

I have always said it is possible to hold two truths at once.
Love and loss.
Longing and letting go.
But I will not be made a casualty of your confusion.

I deserve to feel your care.
I deserve the clarity of your desire.
Not just in whispered moments,
but in the broad daylight of your choosing.

Because I am always vulnerable with you.
Always there.
Always hoping you will rise and meet me whole.

But until then...
I sip my tea.
And sit in my favorite chair.
And hold space for the woman I am—
the one who loves deeply,
who gives freely,
and who, even in pain,
still chooses herself.

Lorna

LETTER NINETEEN

Could You Love This Woman?

Today again,
I sit in my chair.

The steam rises gently from my cup—
a tender jasmine this time,
delicate and fragrant,
reminding me that even the softest blooms
can carry strength in their petals.

And I ask—not as a plea,
but as a woman who knows her worth:

Could you love this woman?

The one who gathers the world in her arms,
who speaks gently even when her voice trembles,
who gives without spectacle,
and serves without needing to be seen.

I am that woman.
The one who does not love halfway.
Who does not dabble in affection like a guest,
but who lays the table, lights the candles,
and says, Come. Rest here.

I love with a heart vast enough
to cradle the pain of strangers
and still save a quiet room for joy.

I rise each morning not just to go,
but to listen.
To feel.
To tend.

I am the one you call
when your world is unraveling.
And I will come.
Not to rescue,
but to sit with you in the ruins
until you remember your own power.

You can trust me.
I will keep your secrets like sacred texts.
I will trace the lines of your sorrow,
not to erase them—
but to understand.

Because I see people.
And I love them in action, not theory.
My love builds clinics in Congo.
My love whispers through the walls
of Ghana's birth rooms.
My love lifts mothers from dirt floors
and wraps their babies in songs

the world has forgotten how to sing.

I am a woman of depth.
Of dignity.
Of devotion.

I read poetry with the same reverence
I read blood pressure charts.
I pack suitcases not to escape,
but to show up—fully, fiercely, and whole.

And yes—
I will cry with you.
And yes—
I will kneel with you.
And yes—
I will walk through fire
if it means you get to feel the sun again.

So, I ask—gently,
but truthfully:

Could you love this woman?

Could you meet her gaze without shrinking from it?
Could you sit with her,
sip tea with her,
and not run from the way her softness breaks you open,
from the way her truth reveals your own?

Because she is here—
tea in hand,
feet planted in purpose,
soul lit like a lantern in the dark.

And she is not asking to be rescued.
She is asking to be met.

Could you love this woman?

Lorna

LETTER TWENTY

Choose You

Today I sit in my chair.
The morning is gentle, and in my hands,
a cup of golden oolong breathes its warmth into me—
smooth, steady, like the rhythm I've had to relearn
after life, and love, and loss.

The light finds me here—
pressing against my cheek like a knowing hand.
And I remember:
I am still here.
Still soft.
Still choosing.

And I chose you.
Not for the grand gestures.
Not for the poetry in your mouth,
but for the quiet ache behind your eyes.
The way your silence said more than your sentences ever could.

I chose you because somewhere in your stillness,
your smile,
your pause before speaking,
I heard the echo of a man who has wept
and learned to walk anyway.

I recognized the grief you carry,
the kind that doesn't introduce itself—
just nestles beneath the ribs and sighs at night.

Still, you showed up.
Still, you tried.

And so, I did not run.
I stayed.
I leaned in.

Even when I wasn't certain.
Even when the tenderness came in drops
rather than downpour.
Even when the romance looked different
than the stories I once held close.

Because something in you
called something in me.
In a world that moves too fast—
that forgets names, forgets hearts—
you stayed long enough for my spirit to remember yours.

I could have held back.
Closed the door gently.
Preserved my solitude.

But I didn't.

Because love,
when given from a full place,
is not weakness.
It is worship.

And I have built a life—
one paved in purpose and calling.
I have spoken in faraway places,
walked through the sacred dust of Ghana and Congo,
stood with mothers and midwives,
sang prayers over newborns,
lit candles in rooms where death once whispered.

I have known purpose that roared like fire.
I have known fear.
I have known glory.

And still—
when your name lit up my phone,
my breath caught.
I answered.
Not because I was waiting.
Not because I needed saving.
But because I recognized
that rarest of things—
a soul crossing.

And I carved out space.
Sacred space.
In a life already overflowing.

That should mean something.

So no, I am not a woman who begs.
I am not a woman who chases.

I am a woman who listens
to the invisible music between two hearts.
I am a woman who pours tea for the ones she sees.
Who honors the mystery of connection.
Who gives with presence, not persuasion.

I chose you.
Deliberately.
Gently.
Without expectation.

And this choosing was holy.

Even now,
with the tea cooling slightly in my hands,
I honor that sacred act.

But let me be honest—
it is not enough.

I wanted it to be.
I wanted what I gave to open something in you.
To stir something eternal.
To teach you the language of devotion
you never learned to speak.

Because what I gave was not casual.
It was not light.
It was sacred.
And it cost me something.
It cost me comfort,
it cost me sleep,
it cost me the softness I had just begun to rebuild.

It caused me pain—
a quiet, dignified pain
that no one could see but me.

And still, I do not regret the choosing.
But I will not stay in a place that does not see me.
I will not keep pouring into an unheld cup.

So today,
I walk away.

I walk away
not bitter,
but bare.

Not angry,
but awake.

I walk away with love in my heart—
but this time, the love is for me.

The kind of love that picks me up,
that wraps me in warm linen,
that whispers: You did not fail,
you felt.
I walk away knowing I honored what was real,
but I will no longer abandon myself to prove it.

I walk away
loving me.

Love,

Lorna

LETTER TWENTY ONE

I See Your Grief,

Even When You Don't Speak It

Today, I sit in my chair—
the one that holds all the versions of me,
the hopeful, the heartbroken, the healing.
And I sip a cup of Golden Monkey.
It is beautiful.
Golden and dark, like liquid silk.
Sweet, with whispers of stone fruit and soft earth.
It comforts. It reminds me that even the bitter can carry beauty.

And today, I write this letter… for you.
You, the man I once loved—and maybe still do—
the man walking through a valley
where even the sun forgets to rise.
You have known grief.
The kind that doesn't knock before entering.
The kind that doesn't leave when you ask it to.
The kind that pitches a tent on your chest
and steals the air from your lungs
every single morning.

A friend once told me that grief is gluttonous.
And I believe her.
Because I have watched it eat everything in you.
Your joy.
Your clarity.
Your desire to be touched.
Even your smile—
that radiant thing that once lit up every room—
has been rationed, like something too sacred to waste.

I see the fog you move through.
I see how you wander through your days like a man haunted,
like someone trying to remember what "okay" used to feel like.
People tell you it will get better.
But what they don't say is when.
Or how.
Or that "better" may not look anything like before.
You nod, you say thank you, but you don't believe it.
Not really.
Because how could you?

They say that when someone dies,
the love doesn't.
And I know this to be true—
you still carry her name in the hollow of your chest.

You still wake up hoping to hear her voice.
You still set the table for two, in your mind.
And sometimes, when you forget
and reach for your phone to call her,
grief crashes down on you all over again—
like a wave that didn't finish its work the first time.

You walk into a house now
where no voice answers back.
Where the silence is not peace,
but punishment.

You look at her clothes still hanging.
Or maybe you've already packed them away,
but even the empty space screams louder than fabric.
Her scent might still cling to a sweater.
Her handwriting still floats on a card tucked in a drawer.
And those small remnants unravel you—
over and over again.

Friends don't know what to say to you,
many don't say anything at all,
or worse, they say too much.
They avoid your eyes because your pain mirrors theirs.
They want you to be "better,"
because your grief reminds them of everything

that can be lost.

And I know—
you keep yourself busy.
You travel.
You work.
You move from place to place like if you keep going,
you can outrun the ache.

But you can't.

Because grief isn't behind you.
It lives with you.
It rides beside you in every car.
Sleeps beside you in every bed.
It waits for you in music, in scent,
in laughter that reminds you of hers.

And I know...
you're trying.

You don't know when or if you'll be ready to love again.
You don't know what "ready" even means.
You go out and you wonder—
is this a date?
Am I betraying her?

Am I rushing?
Am I healing?

You want to be held.
You want to feel the warmth of connection,
but your heart still wears a veil.
You wonder—
can I fall in love too soon?
Can I trust my joy?
And yet, what if I move too slow… and miss the moment?

And so, I say this with all the tenderness I can offer:

I understand your grief.
I understand it better than you think.
I do not wish to rush you.
I do not want to fix what cannot be fixed.
I just want to stand in the gap for you.
To be there—quiet, still, steady—in the corner,
so that when you look around,
you'll know… I have you.
I'm here.

I want to pray for you when you cannot find the words.
I want to hold you when you are tired of being strong.
I will wait for you—

not because I am lost in longing,
but because I believe you are worth it.
Worth it in my love.
Worth it in my life.

And if love finds us again—
if your heart ever chooses to open—
I will be here,
not as a replacement,
but as a reminder that love does not die,
it transforms.

You are not broken.
You are grieving.
And grief is not a weakness.
It is evidence of love that mattered.

Until then,
sip slowly.
Rest often.
Let the world be soft with you.

With tenderness and deep seeing,
For the grieving hearts who still know how to love,

Lorna

LETTER TWENTY TWO

A Man of Substance

Today I sit in my chair.
The one that has held my reflections,
my revelations, my rising.
And in my cup is something bold—
A beautiful black tea from Kenya,
hand-plucked by the women of the highlands.
One bud, two leaves—that's all it takes.
Simplicity and intention.
Strength and grace.
Just like me.

Today, I remember:
I am a woman of worth.
Not because someone says so,
But because I know so.
If there were an ad for me, it would read:

A Woman of Worth
Seeking a Man of Substance.
One who does not shine just in speech,
But in the gentle weight of his walk.

You see, I no longer lean on pretty words alone.
I watch how a man treats me.

That tells me everything.
Because love, real love, is not loud.
It's consistent. It's thoughtful.
It's felt in the way he opens a door,
In how he protects your peace,
In how he checks if you're warm enough,
If you made it home safe,
If the world has been too harsh today—
and he softens it.

The man of substance—
He is always on time,
Not just in presence,
But in purpose.
He speaks with gentleness.
He covers her with intention.
He is not afraid of her light,
Because he carries one of his own.

He will never put her in situations
that feel small or shameful.
He will never dim her.
He will never ask her to fold herself to fit.
Because she can't.
She won't.
She is self-assured.
She is seasoned.
She is stunning—inside and out.
She walks into a room,
And the air shifts.

Even he feels it.
Especially he.

And if she must wait for this man,
So be it.
Because she knows her value.
She knows her presence is rare,
Like the Kenyan tea she sips today—
One bud, two leaves—
Pure. Uncompromised. Intentional.

She will wait, not in longing,
But in becoming.
She fills her days with joy,
Her nights with peace,
Her life with sacred purpose.
And she knows—
The man who is not of substance
Will always be inconsistent.
Because he will always put himself first.
And she has no space in her sacred life for someone
Who cannot see the treasure she is.

So, she waits.
But not idly.
She waits while thriving,
While dancing,
While living in full bloom.
Because the man of substance is not her destination.
He is a companion to her already-whole journey.

And until then…
She sips her tea.
She smiles with her soul.
And she stays rooted in her worth.
With grace,

Lorna

LETTER TWENTY THREE

To the One I Loved: A Prayer from My Chair

Today, I sit in my chair—
the one that knows me best.
The one that has caught my tears,
held my silence,
and witnessed the soft breaking of my heart.

In my hands, I cradle a cup of tea—
warm, fragrant, steady.
I sip slowly, with both palms wrapped around its comfort,
and I offer a prayer for you.

A quiet prayer.
A steady one.
A prayer without bitterness or expectation—
just love, folded gently into breath.

I pray that you are well.
That peace meets you at dawn
and stays with you through every sleepless night.

I pray that sorrow loosens its grip—
the sorrow I saw in your eyes,
felt in your chest,
and sensed in the unseen places

where you've long carried pain.

I have prayed for you for a long time—
and you know that.
Even when the words between us stopped,
my prayers did not.

Even now, as our stories unfold separately,
as our paths diverge,
I still lift your name to the stars.

I pray that God holds you gently in His hand.
That you rediscover your spark—
the one that lights your eyes,
the one that makes your laughter rise from your soul.
I pray you find rest from the restlessness.
That your searching will settle.
That your wondering will give way to wisdom.
I pray joy returns to you—
true joy, the kind that stays without needing a reason.

I pray the air around you is soft.
That the room you sit in holds you with tenderness,
just as this chair holds me now.

And more than anything,
I pray your life becomes full—
full of meaning,
full of light,
full of truth,

full of love.

Because once, I loved you deeply.
And real love—true love—
wants all these things,
even when love changes its form.

So today, I sip my tea.
And I pray.
And I release.

And I send this prayer on the wind to you.

May it find you in perfect time.
May you know you were loved.
Still are.
Always will be.
Love,

Lorna

LETTER TWENTY FOUR

I Claim Elegance and Quiet Things

I sit in my chair and sip tea—
not hurried, not distracted,
but fully present, fully aware,
because simplicity is my sanctuary.
I am a simple woman.
I do not crave chaos or spectacle.
I do not need the noise of the world to feel alive.
Loudness unsettles me.
Vulgarity makes me ache.
I crave what is slow,
what is sacred,
what is still.
Give me a quiet room,
a warm cup,
a gentle breeze through linen curtains.
Let me sit without the need to fill the air.
Let me breathe without explanation.
That is my peace.
I find joy in small things—
the smile of a child,
the curl of steam from the kettle,
a handwritten note,
a hand resting on mine.
I am an elegant woman.

Not by fashion's dictate
but by the grace I carry,
the way I move through this world
with thoughtfulness, with poise.
Elegance lives in my stillness,
in my words that heal,
in the silence I do not fear.
I wear it without apology.
It is not performative—
it is who I am.
I tend to friendships
like gardens that need watering.
I call because I want to hear your voice,
because connection is not a scroll or a screen.
It's the warmth that says, "You matter to me."
It's me asking, "Are you okay?"
It's me listening without needing to fix it.
That's friendship. That's care.
I am not for everyone.
But for those who need a harbor,
a steady voice,
a calm soul in the storm,
I am here.
Today, I stop dimming my light
to make others comfortable.
I stop rushing to fit into spaces
that are too loud for my spirit.
I claim who I am—
a woman of elegance,
a woman of simplicity,

a woman of soft strength.
And I am proud of that.
So very proud.
—The Woman I Am

Lorna

LETTER TWENTY FIVE

Space between the Thought

and I sip a beautiful Earl Grey—
so fragrant, so soft, it curls around me like a morning mist.
The bergamot lifts, floral and citrus,
a perfume that asks nothing but presence.
I breathe in the warmth of the cup,
what does Eckhart Tolle mean
by the space between thought?
It is not silence, exactly.
It is a presence so full,
that it has no need to speak.
It is the moment before the next moment.
The inhale before the word.
The pause where nothing is missing.
I find a stillness that does not cling or grasp—
just the steam rising from my cup,
and the knowing that I am here.
Not thinking, not solving, not remembering—
And perhaps that is what he meant:
that lives between the thoughts.
The sacred space where peace is not earned,
and let the next thought arrive
I sip my tea—a golden turmeric blend, earthy and warm,
with notes of ginger and quiet courage.
It settles in my belly like truth.

No task pulling at my sleeve.
Just this moment—whole, complete,
and asking nothing of me
Practicing the presence is not a ritual of grand gestures.
of the weight of the cup in my hand,
of the way the light rests on the table just so.
It is choosing not to flee the ordinary,
but to fall in love with it.
In the presence, there is no performance.
To be wrapped in the quiet knowing
that this moment is enough.
It is in presence that I meet the Divine—
A nearness too often missed in the rush of doing.
I do not reach for meaning.
I let meaning come to me—
Not perfectly, but honestly.
To practice the presence is to make a home in the now—
and remember that peace is not found later,
or when things are better,
a delicate green jasmine, light as morning fog,
its fragrance like a soft guiding hand resting on my shoulder.
And I think about direction.
About the quiet ache of not knowing the next step,
We all get lost sometimes.
In the endless turning of other people's opinions,
as if their voices were our compass.
steady and unbothered by clouds.
It is about knowing that there is something inside you,
something ancient, that remembers the way—
even when you forget.

It is the dream you shelved long ago.
The truth you whispered into your pillow
when no one else was listening.
The pull you feel in your belly
when you're standing in the wrong place too long.
Your North Star is the yes that lives in your chest.
The holy unrest that says,
"This is not your home. Keep going."
And the beautiful thing is—
you don't have to see the whole map.
You only need to take the next faithful step.
One quiet, intentional step in the direction of what feels right,
but for the sound of my own soul waking up,
finding your North Star is not about finding
something out there—
it's about returning to what's already within.
And remembering you were never really lost.
a deep, earthy oolong with notes of roasted chestnut
and something older still,
something that speaks in the language of memory.
but with the grace of generations.
Women tea farmers, hands weathered and wise,
walking narrow footpaths in mist-covered hills,
plucking leaves like blessings from the bush.
Their quiet labor carried in each steep,
their stories swirling in my cup.
And in this moment, I surrender to stillness.
No demands pulling at the edges of my attention.
Just the breath between sips.
The whisper of steam against my skin.

The quiet recognition of being alive.
It is the space where the soul exhales.
Where truth softens its voice and says,
"I've been here all along. You were just too loud to hear me."
It teaches me that rest is not idleness,
that pause is not weakness,
that silence is a kind of prayer.
I think of the women who came before me—
those who woke before dawn to boil water over open flame,
who harvested leaves with reverence,
who sang while they worked,
whose hands held both grief and beauty with the same strength.
Stillness brings them close.
And I remember that the world does not need more noise.
It needs more women unafraid of the quiet.
It needs more cups poured slowly.
More chairs that hold us like altars.
More afternoons that are not rushed into usefulness.
This is the beauty of stillness.
And the knowing that in this moment—
nothing else is required but breath.
This morning, I sit in my favorite chair—
quiet, worn in the most familiar way.
The sunlight filters through the curtain just right, and in my
hands is a cup of golden tea. It's a delicate jasmine oolong,
lightly floral, with a whisper of earth and honey.
The steam curls up and greets my face. I lift the cup to my lips
and take a slow sip. The warmth is immediate,
a soft bloom across my tongue.
First, the scent reaches me—a breath of spring blossoms.

Then the taste follows: smooth, layered, and alive.
There's a quiet complexity to it, like something that has waited
to unfurl. I close my eyes.
This is not a hurried cup. This is not a morning rushing
out the door. This is a cup for being still, for breathing,
for listening to silence speak.
And as I drink, I think about the waiting.
The prayers that feel unanswered.
The doors that haven't opened.
How often we confuse delay with denial.
But what if the waiting is not punishment—
what if it is protection?
What if it is preparation?
I have learned that waiting is not a void. It is an altar.
A sacred pause. A space where the soul stretches and learns
to trust what it cannot yet see.
The world may say, "You failed."
The mind may whisper, "You're forgotten."
But the heart—the faithful heart—knows to pray differently.
This or something better.
And so, I do not beg. I bless.
I trust that the divine is not delayed, only deliberate.
And if I must wait longer—
May I wait like the tea I drink:
And poured from a place of love.
For in the waiting, I am being made ready.
And the answer is coming—
and more beautiful than I ever imagined.

Lorna

LETTER TWENTY SIX

A Good Reckoning

I sit.
I sip tea.
And for the first time in a long time,
I allow myself a moment
to gather my thoughts,
to re-evaluate,
to reflect.

You know,
our relationship was never what I told myself it was.
It wasn't good from the beginning—
not in the way that truly matters.
It lacked the quality, the depth,
the respect and attention
that I have both given and always known I deserve.

But I stayed.
I stayed because I could see glimpses
of something more in you—
something soft, something kind,
something hidden beneath the heavy layers of grief.
I told myself that once the grief lifted,
you would become the man I imagined,
the man I believed in.
But grief has a way of unearthing

both the beauty and the brokenness in us.
And for you,
it pulled you into survival mode,
operating from a primitive place
where love becomes distant,
and care becomes a shadow of itself.

And so, I made excuses.
I adjusted.
I shrank and stretched,
twisting myself into shapes I didn't recognize—
all in the name of love.
I poured everything into you,
as if making you the king of my castle
would bring me joy.

But you didn't ask for a castle.
You didn't know what to do with the crown.
And in truth,
it was never mine to give.

Now, with time and distance,
I see it all so clearly.
I see how I left myself behind,
how I dimmed my own light
while waiting for you to find yours.

And yet—
this realization is not bitter.
It is not angry.

It is freedom.

I have come to my senses.
I have found my reckoning—
and it is a good reckoning.
One that fills me with peace,
with strength,
with comfort.

Because now,
I know who I am again.
I am a fine lady.

I am a queen in my own right.
And I will never again hand over my crown
to someone who does not know its value.

So today, I sip my tea
and I celebrate this moment of clarity.
I celebrate the beauty of release,
the peace of no longer being tangled
in someone else's storm.

And I feel great—
grateful, even—
that we are no longer in each other's world.
Because now,
I am free to rise in mine.

Lorna

LETTER TWENTY SEVEN

I Come from a Line of Strong Women

I sip tea in my beautiful chair.
And I feel them with me those who walked before,
those whose names echo in the marrow of my bones.
I come from a line of strong women.
I come from Nanny of the Maroons,
warrior of the Jamaican hills,
who fought for freedom with fire in her heart
and strategy in her soul.
I come from Wangari Maathai,
the Kenyan mother of trees,
who planted forests where despair once lived
and dared to stand tall in a world that tried to cut her down.
I come from Rosa Parks,
who sat down in defiance so an entire people could rise.
A quiet storm who changed the course of a nation.
Not just by blood or history but by spirit.
I come from women who resisted in silence and in song.
Women who made healing from herbs, hope from ashes,
and dignity from dust.
Women who were told no—and lived their yes—anyway.
I come to tell you I'm here to change the world.
Not with arrogance, but with purpose.
Not to be famous, but to be faithful.

To the assignment that calls me in the middle of the night
and says: Get up, there is work to do.
I come with stories in my blood and prayers on my tongue.
I come with truth in my hands and love that does not flinch.
So, if you see me quiet, know I am listening.
If you see me still, know I am gathering strength.
If you see me rise, know the ancestors rose with me.
I come from a line of strong women.
And I come to take my place among them.

Lorna

LETTER TWENTY EIGHT

I Sit in My Favorite Chair: The Company I Keep

Today, I sit in my favorite chair.
I drink tea—warm, grounding, familiar.
And I let the quiet settle around me like a shawl,
softening the edges of the day.
not with judgment, but with honesty.
And my thoughts wander to the company I keep.
What do they bring to my soul?
Do they offer joy like sunlight in winter?
Or do they carry with them the sharp edges of tension,
the quiet discomfort that unsettles peace?
Do they walk beside me in reverence—
treating my spirit as something sacred,
not only in words but in actions woven into the everyday?
Do they understand the language of silence,
the way I sometimes retreat to restore myself?
Do they know how to hold space,
to offer care without condition,
presence without pressure?
Do they celebrate my becoming—
my wins, my changes, my growth?
Do they hold me when I am unsure of myself,
and lift me when the weight gets too heavy to carry alone?
Do they tap my shoulder when I grow weary,
not to remind me of what I haven't done,

but to remind me that I am not alone?
Is there partnership in the way they show up?
Is there kindness in the way they speak of me
when I'm not in the room?
Is there honor in how they hold my story?
And in the stillness, I make a vow—
to only make room for those
who bring peace to my table,
who speak truth to my heart,
who walk beside me not out of convenience,
but because they cherish the journey.
I will choose the company I keep
with intention, with warmth,
and with deep gratitude for what fills my cup.
Because this life is sacred.
is the echo of how we love ourselves.

Lorna

LETTER TWENTY NINE

I Am the Prayer of My Ancestors

I Am the Prayer of My Ancestors I sip tea in my beautiful chair. And as the warmth fills my hands, I feel the pulse of something greater—something ancient—beating through me. I am the prayer of my ancestors. I am the answered wish whispered into the night sky.

The sacred dream carried in a woman's womb. The hope they held onto while fields burned, while borders closed, while chains rattled and systems tried to erase them. I am what they could not say out loud but believed with every breath. I am the soft landing after centuries of struggle. I am the freedom they never tasted, living now in my own skin. And because of them— I rise. I speak. I move through this world with the knowledge that my existence is no accident. I am placed. I am purposed. I am patterned from those who survived storms with nothing but spirit. When I speak my truth, I speak for women who were silenced. When I rest, I do so for those who never had the luxury. When I thrive, I do so with reverence—because I know someone long before me paid the cost.

I am not just my name. I am my grandmother's rhythm. My great-grandmother's strength. My great-great-grandmother's resistance stitched into every step I take. And when I doubt myself—when the weight of the world grows heavy and I question whether I am enough— I remember this: I am not just enough—

I am the continuation of a holy story. I walk through this life like a living altar, blessing every space I enter, planting light wherever I go. I don't need a title. My existence is evidence. I am the prayer of my ancestors. And I am becoming everything they hoped I would be.

Lorna

LETTER THIRTY

Let the Soft Life Find You

I sip tea in my beautiful chair. The light is slow this morning. The kind of light that doesn't rush to be anything but what it is. I wonder—what if I gave myself permission to live like that? To stop rushing. To stop proving. To stop surviving like it's the only language I know.

Let the soft life find you. Let it find you when you're done performing for love. Let it find you in the spaces where you no longer feel the need to earn your rest. Let it find you in the sacred hush of a Sunday morning. In linen sheets, quiet rooms, fresh fruit, and long exhalations. Let it find you not because you escaped the hard, but because you've learned that softness is also strength. You were not born to live in fight mode. You were not created just to endure. There is more for you than pain and perseverance. There is beauty. There is gentleness. There is peace. There is tenderness that asks nothing of you but your presence.

Let the soft life be your reward—not for what you've done, but for who you are. Let it hold you. Let it feed you. Let it unclench your jaw and soften your spirit. Let it remind you that hustle is not your worth, and exhaustion is not a badge of honor.

You do not have to live in survival when you were made for bloom. You do not have to prove you've earned softness—

You already have

So, here's to warm tea, long walks, nourishing touch, deep belly laughs, and conversations that feel like a balm. Here's to candles lit for no reason. To slow mornings. To love that doesn't demand a performance. To softness that feels like coming home.

You have survived long enough. Let the soft life find you.
Let it wash over you. Let it stay.

Lorna

LETTER THIRTY ONE

Letter to Myself: I Finally Got It

I sit in my chair—
the one that has held my tears,
my truths,
and the moments when I could no longer pretend.

In my cup, a simple tisane—
peppermint and spearmint.
Cool. Cleansing. Awakening.
A blend made for exhaling,
for letting go,
for coming home to myself.

And today, I say it softly, but surely:
I am done bleeding.

Done bleeding hope for someone
who never asked for healing.
Done bleeding time,
bending backward,
shrinking forward,
waiting sideways for your arrival.

I will not live in hope that you will change.
That hope wore me thin.
That hope unraveled my joy,
thread by thread,
compromise by quiet compromise.

I will not hope for you to surrender your ego,
your silence,
your armor,
and finally meet me where love dwells.
I see now—
that dream was mine, not yours.

I will no longer give you my mornings of overthinking,
my nights filled with breathless prayers,
my years that asked only for tenderness in return.

Because I finally—finally—got it.
I heard the whisper in my spirit say:
Let him go.
You are not his mirror.
You are your own moon.

Now, I am busy.
Busy with the sacred work of me.

I am tending to the woman I once placed on pause.
I am breathing life into the spaces I silenced.
I am planting gardens in my chest.
I am writing psalms on my skin.

I am laughing again.
Sleeping fully.
Walking into rooms as my whole, unhidden self.
And when joy knocks, I open wide and say,
Come in. I've been waiting for you.

You were a chapter.
I closed it gently.
But this—
this is the beginning of my becoming.

Let the tea steep.
Let the peace stay.
Let the woman rise.

Love,

Lorna

LETTER THIRTY TWO

Wanted A Man Who Can Handle A Woman Who Knows Her Power

Today, I sit in my favorite chair, sipping a deep,
smoky cup of Pu-erh—earthy, aged, unapologetically rich.
Just like me.
So, here's my ad:

Unapologetic Woman Seeks a Man Who Can Handle Her.

Not tame her. Not mold her.
Handle her.

A woman who's done the work.
Who walks with purpose, grace, and fire.
Who knows silence can be sacred,
and words can be weapons—so she chooses both wisely.

I am not asking for perfection.
But I am requiring presence.
I require truth.
I require integrity.

You must not be intimidated by brilliance, beauty, or backbone.
You must not crumble under emotion or run from complexity.

I want deep conversation, soulful intimacy, spontaneous
adventure, and quiet Sundays with good tea.

You must know how to hold space—for me, for yourself, for us.
You must understand that I'm not looking to be rescued.
I am looking to be met.

And if you do come…
Come correct.
Come healed.
Come whole.
Or at least, come humble and ready.

This is not for the faint of heart.
But if you've got the courage,
If your soul stirs at the thought of a woman
who leads with her heart and stands in her truth—

Then sit down.
Pour some tea.
Let's talk.

Lorna

LETTER THIRTY THREE

When Destiny Called My Name

Today, I sit in my chair.
The one that has held the weight of my wondering,
the softness of my becoming.
In my cup, I sip beautiful Darjeeling—
golden, floral, kissed by mountain winds.
It calls to me like a memory I never lived,
yet somehow always knew.

And as I sip, I remember the moment Destiny and I met.
It was not loud.
It was not choreographed.
There were no trumpets, no lightning bolts—
just a whisper in my spirit
as I stood barefoot on the edge of the familiar.
I was living in Miami then.
The city buzzed with energy—
all heat and rhythm, motion and shine.
But something ancient stirred in me.
A voice. A hush. A knowing.
It said, Move to DeLand.
And I didn't question.
Because when Destiny speaks,
you don't need clarity—only courage.

So, I moved.
Not to escape,
but to align.
The moment I arrived,
the air felt different.
Gentler. More sacred,
as if it had been waiting for me all along.

I have always worked for myself.
Built my own path, brick by brave brick.
There was no blueprint—only belief.
And somehow, through every risk,
through every turn in the road,
Destiny kept showing up—
quiet, constant, undeniable.

You came into my life,
and though I may never fully understand the why,
I believe you were sent to teach me something.
Perhaps to remind me to pause,
to soften,
to open myself again to the sweetness of love.
Perhaps to hold up a mirror to the woman I've become.

Because everything—everything—
has been divinely arranged.
Every meeting.
Every leaving.
Every place I laid my head.
Every tear and triumph.

Nothing was wasted.

I was born for a time like this.
I know that now.
For this voice.
This calling.
This sacred way of being.

Destiny is not a destination.
She is a rhythm.
A song beneath my skin.
She does not shout.
She does not beg.
But when she moves,
she moves mountains.

One day, Destiny and I met.
She looked like me—
older, wiser, certain.
And she smiled,
as if to say:
You listened.
You trusted.
And now, beloved,
you are exactly where you're meant to be.

So, I sip this Darjeeling,
tea kissed by sky and soil,
and I give thanks for every invisible thread
that wove this life into something so true,

so bold,
so beautifully mine.

Peace and promise,

Lorna

LETTER THIRTY FOUR

Letter to Self – Sweet Surrender

My Beloved Self,
This morning, I sit in my chair—
the one that has held every version of me.
The morning light slips through the curtains,
and my cup of tea is warm in my hands,
its steam curling like a gentle prayer toward the ceiling.
The house is quiet.
I believe I am alone.
Then, suddenly, a voice.
I freeze for a moment,
startled—but not afraid.
Startled because I know this home,
I know this silence,
and I was not expecting another presence.
But this voice… oh, this voice.
It is familiar.
It does not frighten.
It feels like love wearing sound.
It moves through the room the way sunlight
moves across water—
gentle, undeniable, certain.
All is going to be okay, it says.
And I believe it.
I have come to know this voice over the years.

It has visited me in the ache of my heartbreak
and in the quiet hours when the world felt heavy.
It is the voice of the Divine.
The voice of Spirit.
The voice of my own soul in conversation with God.
It always speaks softly,
but its words land like anchors of truth in my heart.
Your perfect person is on the way, it whispers.
Trust the timing.
Tend to your health.
Tend to your soul.
Self-care is not a luxury—it is holy.
Your healing matters.
Prepare yourself.
Because when love comes,
you must be ready to receive it fully,
without hesitation,
without the weight of old wounds holding you back."
I listen.
I do not interrupt with my worries or my what-ifs.
I do not ask the questions that once would have burned in me:
Will it be the love I once held,
or a new love I have never met?
Will it be a familiar hand or a stranger's smile?
I do not ask,
because I do not need the details.
When Heaven speaks,
the details are the least important thing.
What matters is the knowing.
And I know this voice as surely as I know my own breath.

So, I sit back in my chair,
the warmth of my tea curling through my fingers,
and I surrender.
Sweet surrender.
I let the tension fall from my shoulders.
I let my heart unclench.
I let anticipation replace anxiety,
because I can feel something beautiful approaching my life.
Not the frantic kind of waiting,
not the restless pacing of someone desperate for answers,
but the kind of waiting that feels like standing in the morning sun,
knowing light will reach your skin if you simply stay still.
In this surrender, joy rises.
I feel alive,
tingling with quiet excitement.
I can almost feel the edges of the life that is coming for me—
a life where love meets me openly,
where laughter fills rooms I haven't yet walked into,
where my heart is safe to bloom again.
Until then, I tend to myself.
I honor my own becoming.
I drink my tea and nourish my body.
I speak kindly to my reflection.
I move my body with gratitude.
I care for my spirit the way I once cared for everyone else.
Because the voice has taught me this:
Love arrives most fully
when you are already loving yourself well.
The great romance begins with the woman in the chair,

the one who has learned to be whole on her own.

So, I wait.
In grace.
In joy.
In faith that does not waver.
My beloved self,
one day soon, love will arrive,
and it will find you ready—
not because you chased it,
not because you begged for it,
but because you made space for it,
because you honored yourself enough to prepare.
Until that day,
sip your tea.
Breathe deeply.
Keep healing.
Keep shining.
And remember, always remember:
Heaven has already whispered—
All is well.

With devotion and hope,

Me,

Lorna

LETTER THIRTY FIVE

Never Ever Settle

A Letter to the One I Love
I sit in my chair—
the one that has carried me through reckoning and revelation.
Steam rises from my tea,
a fragrant reminder to slow down,
to listen to what I already know.

I know this:
I will never, ever settle.

Not for halfway love.
Not for affection that flickers when it's convenient.
Not for breadcrumbs when I was born for banquet.

I will not settle for someone
who cannot see the sacredness of my presence.
For someone who turns their face away
from the brilliance of my becoming.

I will never settle for being tolerated.
I am meant to be cherished.
Held in truth.
Loved in full bloom.

I will not twist myself into someone else's shape
to make them comfortable.
I am not here to be a quiet echo in someone else's life.
I am the whole sound.
I am the symphony.

And you—
you, the one I love—
must rise to meet me where I stand,
not ask me to shrink so you can feel tall.

Because even in longing,
even in silence,
even in the late hours when doubt tries to slip in,
my heart has always known what it deserves.

And that knowing has become my guide.
So I wait.
Not from fear.
Not from lack.
But from power.

I wait with grace.
With joy.
With a fierce kind of softness.

I wait for the one who does not flinch at my fire,
but stands in it with reverence.
I wait for the one who arrives with both hands open—
not to take,

but to give.
To meet.
To build.

I wait for the day my heart says:
This is safe.
This is sacred.
This is mine.

And until then,
I sip my tea.
I love my life.
And I bloom, unapologetically.

Love,

Lorna

LETTER THIRTY SIX

Walk Away

My chair.
My tea.
And this much I know:

Walk away.

Walk away from love that never truly held you.
Walk away from love that no longer sees you.
Walk away from the illusion—
the kind of love that drains instead of pours.

Walk away from the selfish one—
the one who takes and rarely gives,
who listens only to speak,
who makes you feel lonelier in partnership
than you ever did in solitude.

Walk away when your heart whispers,
This is not the one.
Walk away when your soul stiffens at their presence.
Walk away when something in you flinches,
even as they offer a smile.

Walk away when trust becomes fragile,

when truth feels out of reach,
when your intuition folds itself into a quiet warning
you keep trying to ignore.

You already know.
You know it in your bones.
You know it in the quiet ache beneath your laughter.
You know it in the spaces where joy used to live.

And yes—
it will hurt.
It will tear something open.
It will feel like a kind of dying.

But still—
walk away.

Because peace is better than pretending.
Because joy should never be bartered for silence.
Because your spirit deserves a place to rest,
not to wrestle.

Walk away.
You'll cry.
You'll wonder.
You'll ache.

But one day—
one holy day—
you'll breathe again.

And in that breath,
you will find yourself.

Whole.
Wiser.
Unshakeable.
Love,

Lorna

LETTER THIRTY SEVEN

The Waiting

This morning, I sit in my favorite chair.
The one that knows the curve of my back,
the rhythm of my breath,

the woman I am when I am not performing—just being.
Sunlight spills gently through the curtain,
and in my hands is a cup of golden tea.
Jasmine oolong.
Delicate. Floral. A whisper of earth and honey.

The steam rises like prayer.
I bring the cup to my lips and sip slowly.
This tea is not for rushing.
It is for reverence.
For stillness.
For listening to the quiet voice of the soul.

As I drink, I think about the waiting.
The space between what I asked for and what has yet to arrive.
The dreams that feel deferred.
The doors that have not opened.
The prayers that echo back silence.

I no longer confuse delay with denial.

I no longer see waiting as punishment.

Now, I see it for what it truly is:
An altar.
A sacred pause.
A space where my soul stretches,
strengthens, softens, and grows.
The world may say, You missed your chance.
The mind may whisper, You're forgotten.
But I have learned to pray differently.

This or something better.
This or someone greater.

So I do not beg. I bless.
I do not grasp. I release.
I do not fear. I trust.

Because the Divine is not delayed—only deliberate.

And if I must wait longer,
may I wait like the tea I drink:
steeped in stillness,
infused with patience,
and poured from a place of love.

I know this truth now:
In the waiting, I am being made ready.
And what is meant for me—
will arrive on time,

in full,
and more beautiful than I ever imagined.

Love,

Lorna

LETTER THIRTY EIGHT

The Woman of Worth

My tea is calling me.
Soft steam rises like a prayer.
And my chair calls too—
that sacred, familiar place
that holds all my questions,
even the ones I've never dared to ask.

Today, I sit in wonder.
Not worry—
but wonder.

I think of Maslow—
of the slow, aching climb up the mountain of self.
Of the layers of unmet needs,
the dreams deferred,
the pieces gathered.

First, I longed for safety.
Then I longed for love.
Then I found my voice.
And now—
now I long to become.

I want to be self-actualized.

To stretch wide into my purpose.
To live not from survival,
but from sacred expression.

To be a woman no longer shrinking,
no longer folding herself
to be digestible,
to be chosen,
to be understood.

I want to live in the truth of who I am—
not the performance,
not the projection,
but the rooted, radiant self
who dances barefoot in her calling,
who speaks even when her voice trembles,
who creates, gives, leads,
and loves from the overflow.

Still, the questions whisper:
Can I be all of this—
and still be loved?

Can I grow and not lose
those who said they loved me
hen I was smaller?

Can I rise and still be held?
And the answer floats up,
like steam from my cup:

Yes, beloved. Yes.

You do not have to shrink for love.
You do not have to silence your brilliance
or slow your healing
to be embraced.

There is love that will not fear your fullness.
There is partnership that will water your roots
and bless your bloom.

There is someone who will not only allow you to rise—
they will rise beside you.

There is someone who will stand and cheer for you,
someone who will watch you on stage with stars in their eyes
and pride in their voice.

They will tell you:
You are beautiful. You are brilliant. You are loved.
And they will mean every word.

So, become.
Don't wait.

Build.
Write.
Create.
Expand.

Speak your name in full syllables.
Drink your tea with reverence.
And know—
the one who is meant for you
will not find you in your hiding,
but in your becoming.

Love,

Lorna

LETTER THIRTY NINE

I Sit in My Favorite Chair

tea warm between my palms,
its steam rising like a prayer—
soft, sacred, sure.

And in this stillness, I feel it:
I am at peace.
I am full.
I am deeply, wholly satisfied with the life I've lived.

Not just a life of accolades,
but a life of alignment.
A life stitched together with purpose,
threaded with service,
and crowned with quiet joys.

I love who I am.
I love how I love.
And all of this—
every inch of this radiant becoming—
existed before you ever entered the room.

So understand this:
I am not searching for someone to complete me.
I have already done the soul's hard work—

the gathering, the healing, the remembering.

What I desire now is sacred partnership.
Not rescue. Not performance.
But presence.
Intentional, conscious, rooted love.

I long for someone who honors my fire
and welcomes my softness,
who watches how I carry the world
and says, Let me carry some too.

Someone who delights in my voice,
respects my silence,
and meets me with proud eyes and open hands.

Let us laugh freely,
speak honestly,
disagree kindly,
and hold space gently.

I don't need a savior.
I simply long to be met.
Truly met—
with reverence, with joy,
and with the courage to build something beautiful together.

And until then—
this moment, this chair, this tea,
reminds me of a deeper truth:

I have already arrived.

Lorna

LETTER FORTY

Food as Soul Ceremony

Today, I sit in my chair,
and in my cup is Dragon Well—Longjing—
one of the finest green teas in the world.
The leaves are smooth and flat, hand-pressed and kissed by fire.
Its flavor is soft—nutty, clean, almost sweet.
It tastes like stillness, like discipline, like devotion.
And that is how I choose to live.

I have come to know food not as routine,
but as ritual.
Food is sacred. Food is soul work.

I don't snack.
I don't reach for sugars.
I don't eat to fill time or distract from feeling.
I eat to nourish.
To align.
To remember who I am.

I follow a holistic path—
intuitive, intentional, alive.
I love raw foods:
sun-blushed tomatoes,
vibrant kale that crackles with life,

zucchini ribbons, ruby beets,
herbs torn gently by hand.
Juices pressed fresh—green and glowing—
like liquid light.

I don't live in chaos, and neither does my kitchen.
My counters are clean,
a reflection of the calm I insist upon.
Because wholeness doesn't live in clutter.
It lives in clarity.
And every night, without fail, I return to the stove—
not for anyone else,
but for me.

You'll find me preparing a meal with care,
chopping with rhythm, seasoning with reverence.
And when it's ready,
I plate it like art—
ladled beautifully, lovingly,
as if royalty were about to dine.

Because I am the royalty.
This body is the temple.
This moment, the offering.

I set the table just for me.
Cloth napkin.
Real silverware.
A bloom in a jar.
And I sit—fully present—at the altar of my own nourishment.

I savor every bite.
I chew with intention.
And my soul sings.

And when I go out,
yes, I love fine dining—
but not in grand, impersonal halls.
I seek small, intimate restaurants
where the soul of the chef comes through on every plate.
Where the music is soft and the lighting low,
and the food tells you a story before your first taste.

And when the chef is a woman—
doing soulful, different, daring things with food—
my heart smiles.
Because I see her.
I feel her.
Her hands, her choices, her joy and struggle—
all of it, poured into the dish.
It touches the deepest part of me.
It feels like communion.
It feels like coming home.

Because food is never just about food.
It's about presence.
About wholeness.
About honoring life bite by sacred bite.

Lorna

LETTER FORTY ONE

Dream a Bigger Dream

Today I sit in my favorite chair, wrapped in stillness and the sacred fragrance of Mindfulness tea, a Desert Sage blend of Assam, malva flower, and corn flower, smooth and grounding, earthy and wise. Whether hot or cold, it settles me into my bones, whispers to my spirit, You are safe. You are here. You are ready.

And today, I speak truth to myself:
It is time to dream a bigger dream.
Not the kind of dream that fits inside a notebook.
Not the kind you whisper under your breath, so you don't scare it away. But the kind of dream that stretches your wings, that rises like sun-warmed mist off a lake at dawn—a dream that terrifies and electrifies you all at once.

I write this letter to remind you:
You were not born to play small. You were not made for just enough. You were crafted from stardust and ancestral fire, from prayers whispered by women who survived
more than you'll ever know. And because of them,
you get to be bold.
So how do you begin?

Step one:
Recommit to yourself.
Recommit to your deepest truth.
What brings you alive?
What breaks your heart open?
Follow that. Pour into it. Protect it.
Your dream will always be connected
to what makes your soul burn bright.

Step two:
Write it down—without censorship.
Let it spill out like poetry, wild and messy.
Don't shrink it to fit the expectations of others.
Don't filter it through practicality.
Write it like you believe God is watching and nodding in approval.

Step three:
Surround yourself with dream-midwives.
Find those who fan your flames, not smother them.
Those who say, "Yes, I see it too," when you describe the vision.
Let go of anyone who calls your dream foolish.
Not everyone is meant to walk with you to the mountain.

Step four:
Act like it's already yours.
Speak like it. Dress like it. Show up like it.
Prepare room for it in your life.
Take one bold step every day.
Even baby steps count. Especially those.

Step five:
Trust divine timing and your own worthiness.
Stop thinking you must "earn" this dream.
You are already worthy of the stage, the impact, the beauty, the reach.
You are enough now.
You are chosen now.
The dream chose you as much as you chose it.

And finally—
Dreaming big is not just about you.
It's about the ripple.
It's about the lives you'll touch, the doors you'll open,
the women who will rise because they saw you rise.
So, sip your tea, daughter of the vision.
Let the warmth fill you.
Let the taste remind you of your strength and softness.
And dare to say it out loud:

I am dreaming a bigger dream. I am ready.
With fire and gentleness,
—Me
A woman becoming whole, one sacred step at a time.

Affirmation
I am whole.
I am radiant in my becoming.
I do not chase love—I attract what aligns with my truth.
The love I seek is sacred, intentional, and rooted in reciprocity.
I am worthy of a partnership that honors the fullness of who I am.

I do not shrink to be chosen. I rise to be met.
I am already home within myself.
And from this place of peace,
I open my heart to what is meant for me.

Love,

Lorna

LETTER FORTY TWO

Love Finds Me in My Cup

So, another morning is here.
And I sit in that chair—the same chair I sit in every morning.
The one that holds the shape of my body and the rhythm
of my breath. The one that has come to know my quiet sighs,
my hopes, my whispered prayers.

Tea in hand. Silence all around. And a question rises like steam:
Will love ever find me?
Are some people simply born to walk this world without it?
Is love a gift for some and not for others?

I do not rush to answer. Instead, I sip. Slowly. Reverently.

And in that sip, I remember.

I remember that I give love—freely, constantly, without
condition.
And I remember that love finds me too—in unexpected ways,
in sacred encounters, in the grace of a sunrise or the laughter of a
friend. Love comes quietly sometimes, not in grand declarations
but in soft gestures: a warm cup, a remembered name, a shared
moment of stillness.

And I remember this truth:

An open heart will always invite love.
A heart willing to stay soft in a hard world
will always be magnetic.

The Divine has not forgotten me. No, the Divine has steeped my life in something tender and profound. In this extraordinary opportunity to savor tea from every corner of the world. To taste the lands. To honor the hands—especially the hands of women who pick these leaves. Women who are often unseen. Often unnoticed.

But I see them. I honor them.

And in that honoring, I find love.

In every sip, I find love.
In every cup, I find comfort.
In this moment, I find gratitude.

So yes, love finds me.
In the warmth of this tea.
In the sacred quiet of my chair.
And most of all, in the open chamber of my heart.

Love,

Lorna

LETTER FORTY THREE

Letter to Myself: The Wind Carries Me

Letter to Myself: The Wind Carries Me
Today I sit in my chair—
the one that knows my name,
the one that has held my weeping,
my wisdom,
and the slow unfolding of my becoming.

In my hands, I cradle a cup of Lapsang Souchong—
smoky, deep, mysterious,
like the memory of a fire that once kept me warm.
And just then—
the wind comes.

Soft at first, then stronger,
strong enough to stir the settled places of my soul.
She wraps herself around me like a shawl,
like a mother's hands,
and I hear her whisper:

My daughter, I carry you.
Your dreams are in the wind.
I will take your sorrow now.
Let it be carried. Let it be lifted.

The wind.
How sacred she is.

In the wisdom of Native tradition,
she is the breath of the ancestors.
A holy messenger.
A spirit that moves between worlds.
To the Lakota, the wind is the Great Spirit's breath.
In the East, she is Prana—
life force.
Movement.
Freedom.

The wind is not just weather.
She is energy.
She is voice.
She is presence.
She is freedom.

And today—
she comes for me.

She does not ask me to be more.
She does not ask for perfection or performance.
She only whispers what I already know:

You are whole.
You did the work.
You faced yourself in silence.
You healed.

You are ready.

Ready for a love that honors.
A love that does not shrink or silence.
A love that stays.
That lifts.
That breathes beside you, not over you.

And in this moment—
I feel my joy.

Not performative.
Not borrowed.
Not waiting for someone else to ignite it.
But mine.
Rooted.
Radiant.
Free.

I thank the wind
for carrying what I could no longer hold.
For whispering truths I had forgotten.
For becoming the mirror I needed.

And I say thank you—
to the one whose love could not stay.
To the story that unraveled.
To the ending that came too soon.

Thank you.

Thank you for being part of my turning.
Thank you for teaching me the art of letting go.
Because even in the undoing,
I found myself.

Even when love faltered,
I rose.
I learned.
I loved anyway.
And now I sit—
tea in hand,
wind in my hair,
gratitude in my chest.

I am a better woman.
A whole woman.
A healed woman.

And for this—
I bow to the wind.
I bow to the path.
I bow to myself.

Let the wind carry it.
Let love find you.
You are ready now.
Love,

Lorna

LETTER FORTY FOUR

Letter to Myself: Loving Is Worth It.

I sit with my tea.
I sip slowly, reverently.
And the truth comes to me—
not like a storm,
but like sunlight warming my skin
after too many cold mornings.

It finds me.
Softly.
Surely.

And I smile—
a smile that rises not from the lips,
but from the soul.
The kind of smile that knows something
sacred has just been remembered.

I exhale.
A beautiful, full-bodied sigh—
the kind that releases what no longer belongs,
and makes space for truth to settle in.

And the truth is this:
Loving is worth it.

It fills your heart.
It stretches your lungs with joy.
It softens your voice and lights your skin from the inside out.

When you love,
you move differently.
You laugh with your whole chest.
You hum without realizing it.
You remember that life is not just survival or lists—
it is moments.
And love, in all its forms,
is one of the most beautiful ones.

Love shows up in your eyes.
In how you hold the door open.
In how you hope.
In how you care.
In how you stay tender
even after goodbye.

So whether love lasts a moment,
a month,
a lifetime,
or lives on in memory—
loving is worth it.

Not just for the outcome.
But for what it awakens in you.
For how it returns you to yourself.
For how it reminds you

of your extraordinary capacity to feel.

To love is to live.
To love is to be brave.

And I am both.

Today, I sit with my tea.
And I honor every love that passed through me—
the gentle ones,
the wild ones,
the ones that broke me open,
and the ones that stitched me whole.

Each one a thread in my becoming.
Each one a gift.

And I smile—
because love was never the mistake.
It was always,
always,
a sacred offering.

Love,

Lorna

LETTER FORTY FIVE

Grateful for the Becoming

I sit in my beautiful chair,
the one that has known my shape,
held my silence,
and caught my exhale after the storms.
This chair has hugged me through seasons—
the blooming and the breaking,
the doubting and the dawning.
It does not judge.
It simply receives me
as I am.

In my hands, I cradle a warm cup of tea—
a quiet companion,
a balm,
a daily baptism.

Today, the tea is soft and earthy,
like autumn leaves on forest ground.
It carries the memory of mountain winds
and the hands of women who plucked it
with reverence and rhythm.
It is not just tea.
It is healing.

I sip slowly.
Each breath is a prayer,
each pause a note in the song of my becoming.
This ritual—this sacred sitting, this slow sipping—
has saved me.

It has taught me how to come home to myself,
how to listen to the ache without fleeing,
how to hold grief in one hand
and gratitude in the other.

Here, in this stillness,
I have learned many lessons.

I have learned that survival is not the same as living.
That love is not something you chase—
it is something you embody.
That peace is not given—
it is cultivated, moment by moment, breath by breath.
And that no one, not even the one you loved most,
can complete you.
Only you can do that.

And so,
today,
I am grateful.

Grateful for the experience—
every high, every fall, every unraveling.
Grateful for the tears that baptized my strength.

Grateful for the laughter that reminded me
joy is not a destination,
but a choice made daily.

Grateful for loving you—
yes, even you.
Even if the love didn't last.
Even if the ending stung like winter wind.
Because loving you taught me
about the depth of my capacity to feel,
to open,
to risk the trembling softness of my heart.

And that love,
no matter how it ended,
was holy,
because it led me back to me.

And most of all,
I am grateful for the woman I have become.

She no longer measures her worth
by who stays or who leaves.
She no longer begs for crumbs
when she is the whole feast.

She has learned to bless the mirror.
To speak her name like a prayer.
To dance barefoot in her own truth.
To rise without apology.

She has made peace with the past.
She has kissed her scars and named them sacred.
She has wept, and she has worshiped,
and she has whispered yes to herself
a thousand quiet times.

This woman,
the one I am now,
she is the one I prayed to become
when I didn't know if I would make it.

And this tea, this chair, this morning—
they are witnesses to the miracle.

The miracle of healing.
The miracle of becoming.
The miracle of stillness
that carries no shame.

I am not broken.
I am not waiting.
I am not small.

I am whole.
And I am home.

Lorna

LETTER FORTY SIX

I Have a Purpose

I sip my tea,
and I sit in my beloved chair—
the one that holds me like an old hymn,
soft and unwavering.
And today…

I am filled with joy.

Not the fleeting kind,
not the kind that depends on a person
or a moment or a headline.
But the deep kind.
The kind that bubbles up from the marrow of my bones.
The kind that makes me want to shout,
want to dance barefoot in the living room,
want to lift my hands to the sky
and say thank you.

Because today—
I remember.

I remember that I was born on purpose,
for a purpose.
That I carry something holy inside of me.

That no one else on this earth
can do exactly what I was born to do.
I have a purpose.

It is not always grand and loud.
Sometimes, it is quiet as a whisper.
Sometimes, it shows up in how I love,
in how I sit and listen,
in how I speak truth into broken spaces.
Sometimes, purpose looks like staying.
Sometimes, it looks like leaving.
Sometimes, it looks like resting
so I can rise again.
But always—always—
it is mine.

And that knowing?
It frees me.

It frees me from comparison.
From the need to explain myself.
From the pressure to be like her
or to follow their path,

because I have my own.

And even if no one else sees it,
even if the applause never comes,
even if the world tries to convince me otherwise—
I know.

And that is enough.
My life is not an accident.
My voice is not background noise.
My dreams are not too big.
My presence is not too much.

I am here for something real.
Something meaningful.
Something eternal.
And so I sip my tea,
and I sit in my chair,
and I say with all the fire in my chest—
I have a purpose.
I am finally ready
to walk in it
with joy,
with clarity,
and with no apology.

Lorna

LETTER FORTY SEVEN

I Lay That Burden Down

I sit.
I sit with my tea.
I sit in my chair, the one that holds my soul
like an old friend,
the one that knows the shape of my heartbreak,
the rhythm of my breath,
the curve of my back when I've bent too long
beneath the weight of it all.

And today,
I make a sacred decision.
I decide to put it down.

All of it.

The confusion that clouded my days.
The chaos that tangled up my joy.
The uncertainty that pulled me into restless nights.

The coming and not coming.
The texts, the silence, the waiting.
The wondering if I did too much,
or not enough.
The hoping that maybe tomorrow would be different.

The dreaming of a version of us that only lived in my head.
The projecting.
The believing that love must be earned, must be suffered for.
The desperate desire to make sense of it all.

I put it all down.
Not because I no longer care—
but because it was never mine to carry.
I was holding something that didn't want to be held.
Nurturing something that refused to grow.
Chasing a truth that would never come honestly.

Today, I set it gently on the altar of release.
No anger.
No bitterness.
Only the deep, clean breath of letting go.

I reclaim my time.
I reclaim my softness.
I reclaim my worth.
I take the energy I spent on waiting—
and pour it back into myself.
Back into the woman I am becoming.
Back into the dreams that are still waiting for me.
Back into my joy, my light,
my future.
I do not need a final word,
a tidy ending,
a neat little bow.

My freedom is not dependent on anyone else's clarity.
My healing does not require their remorse.
I am allowed to move forward—without explanation.

So, I rise.
And as I take another sip from my cup,
I feel it.

Peace.

Not because everything is fixed,
but because I am no longer trying to fix what was never mine.
I am simply choosing myself.
Today, I lay that burden down.
And I walk away—lighter.

Lorna

LETTER FORTY EIGHT

Today, I Feel Divine

Today I sit in the wonderful chair that has known all of me—
my dreaming, my healing, my soft returns.
And in my cup? Moroccan Mint.
Oh, Moroccan Mint—
sweet, bright, kissed with history and mystery.
It dances with the spirit of North Africa,
with desert winds and sacred whispers.
It is bold, fresh, and awakening.
Just like me today.

Today, I feel special.
Today, I feel divine.
There's something in the air, something in my being.
I woke up remembering who I am—
a daughter of grace,
a woman wrapped in the love of God,
a soul that is allowed to soar.

Later…
I will step into the sanctuary of my spa.
Not just a place—but a sacred space.
A temple where I return to myself.
Steam will rise like incense.
The sauna will silence the noise.

Red lights will bathe me in renewal.
And gentle hands will knead away all tension.

There will be a facial to brighten my skin,
a manicure to remind my hands of beauty,
a pedicure to kiss the ground I walk upon.
Because today, I honor my body.
Because today, I honor my soul.
Because today, I remember:

I am divine.
I am worthy of this tenderness.
I am a child of God,
and I am allowed to feel like I could fly.

And oh—how I do.

Lorna

LETTER FORTY NINE

The Third Act

Today I sit in my favorite chair—
the one that has rocked my sorrow,
held my dreams,
and steadied me through every transformation.
And in my cup is Gyokuro,
a rare and precious green tea from Japan—
shade-grown, delicate, and filled with quiet depth.
It is smooth, almost sweet,
like a whispered blessing on the tongue.
It reminds me of what it means to be cultivated in the dark,
only to emerge more luminous than ever.

Yes, today I sip Gyokuro,
and I know—I know—
I am in my Third Act.

The Third Act…
It is not a winding down.
It is a rising.
It is the chapter where the woman becomes the masterpiece.
Where wisdom meets wonder.
Where all the tears, all the lessons, all the grace
come together and write something magnificent.

In the Third Act,
I no longer shrink.
I no longer ask permission.
I no longer apologize for my brilliance,
my softness, or my boundaries.

In the Third Act,
I dress for joy,
I speak with power,
I love without fear,
and I walk like the whole world is watching—
because it is.

I feel it deep in my spirit today:
Favor is finding me.
Doors are opening in rooms I have not yet entered.
Hearts are softening in places where I was once unseen.
Love—real love—is turning toward me with recognition
in its eyes.
My body is vibrant.
My purpose is clear.
My soul is no longer hiding behind old wounds.

This life—this beautiful, glorious, spectacular life—
is mine to live boldly, deliciously, freely.
I am not chasing anything anymore.
I am attracting it all.

Because in this Third Act,
I have remembered who I am.

A daughter of divine favor.
A woman of radiant becoming.
A light in full bloom.

So I lift my cup of green tea,
and I sip slowly,
knowing—
All is well.
And all shall be well.

Lorna

LETTER FIFTY

A Letter to My Future Self

I sit in my chair, as I often do.
Cradling my tea.
Letting the warmth travel through my hands,
into my chest, into the softest, most hopeful part of me.

And today, I write to you—
my future self.

To the woman you are becoming, the woman I am learning
to love more deeply with each passing day, the woman I am
preparing this life for—
I see you.
I honor you.
I speak your name with tenderness
I wish you joy.
Unapologetic, unfiltered joy.
The kind that makes you laugh out loud
in the middle of nowhere, at the most unexpected time,
because life is that good.

I wish you happiness.
Not the kind that is fleeting or performative,
but the quiet, steady happiness
that follows you like the scent of jasmine

on a breezy morning—
delicate, constant, yours.

I wish you abundance.
In all things that matter:
love, health, peace, purpose, the ability to give and receive,
to open your hands to life
and never feel like you have to clutch or beg.

I wish you amazing health.
The kind of vitality that lets you dance barefoot
in the kitchen,
run through new cities without pain,
wake up each morning and feel your body say,
Yes, we're ready for today.
I wish you travel.
To places that stir your soul,
to lands where your name is unknown,
but your spirit is recognized.
I hope you speak new languages with your eyes,
and carry stories in your footsteps.

I wish you laughter.
So much laughter that your eyes water
and your belly aches, and you thank the heavens
for moments that remind you of your aliveness.

I wish you dancing.
Alone. With friends. In candlelight. In moonlight.
With strangers who become family.

May your hips always remember joy.

But above all, my dear future self—
I wish you love.
Not the kind that flickers and fades,
but the kind that endures.
The kind of love that sits with you
in your silence, holds you in your chaos,
and hugs you like it was born to.

A love that sees you.
Really sees you—
before the makeup, beyond the resume,
beneath the titles.

A love that anticipates your needs
before you even speak them.

Someone who sends you flowers and perfume
not because it's your birthday,
but because it's Tuesday
and they thought of you
while the wind carried your name.

Someone who takes you to beautiful dinners
and stares at you like you are the art.

Someone who calls you beautiful—
and means it.
Someone who listens.

Someone who stays.
Someone you trust.

Someone who holds your dreams with reverence.
Who sees your power and does not fear it.
Who creates a home with you,
not just of walls and furniture,
but of shared breath and open hearts.

Someone who does not complete you,
because you are already whole—
but who walks beside you
because they know you were never meant to walk alone.
That is what I desire for you.

So drink your tea, trust the journey,
and know that everything you are hoping for
is already reaching for you too.

You are not behind.
You are not forgotten.
You are becoming.
And I am proud of you already.
With all the love I have,
Me
Today I sit in my chair.

Lorna

LETTER FIFTY ONE

Circle of Women

I sip slowly—white tea from the high gardens of Nepal.
Delicate. Simple.
Because I need clarity.
Because my spirit is calling for truth.

Today I am calling the women together.
My strong sisters.
My seers and singers.
My givers and guardians.
We are gathering.
In a circle.
We are calling the ancestors.
We are lighting candles,
And we are speaking truth to power.

We are remembering what we have forgotten—
That we are sacred.
That our availability is not a gift to be tossed to anyone
Who dials our number when he's lonely.
We speak the truth that says:
Do not always be the available one.

If every time he calls—no matter how long it's been—
You answer.

You show up.
You rearrange your peace.
You dim your boundaries.
You are slowly abandoning yourself.

And you, beloved, are not meant to be abandoned.
Not by anyone.
And certainly not by you.

We must teach with our choices.
We must model respect with our silence.
With our "No."
With our "Not this time."
With our absence.

And it might mean we lose him.
Yes.
Because he doesn't understand.
Because he doesn't know how to hold a woman like you.
Because he's never learned sacred communion—
The kind that holds space,
That listens deeply,
That honors presence.

But that is his journey.
Not yours.

Today, in this circle, we share stories—
Of love that almost broke us,
Of leaving when it hurt,

Of rising when we thought we couldn't.
We cry. We laugh. We remember who we are.

And we make a vow:
That we will always, always put ourselves first.
That we will demand respect.
That we will honor the temple that is our life.
And that we will always be prepared to walk away
from anything,
from anyone
that asks us to shrink.
That dares to treat us as less than divine.

Because we are women.
Powerful.
Worthy.
Whole.

And today,
We drink tea and tell the truth.
We circle up.
And we come back to ourselves.
With fierce love,

Lorna

LETTER FIFTY TWO

The Story Is Mine to Tell

The Story Is Mine to Tell
Today, I sit in my chair,
the one that has held me through quiet reckonings
and riotous awakenings.
In my cup, a beautiful Hochija —
toasted, fragrant, with whispers of smoke and honey.
It tastes like a story steeped in fire
and softened by time.
And that is how I feel today—
like a story the world tried to edit,
but I rewrote in my own hand.

Sister, there will be moments
when they try to write you wrong.
When they narrate your name in half-truths,
mislabel your silence as surrender,
and decorate your pain with shame.

But hear me now—
You must own your story.
Even the chapters you whispered in the dark.
Even the ones you burned
in the backyard of your memory.
Even the ones that never got a fair ending.

Because you are the only one
who can tell it in full color,
with truth, with texture, with grace,
with the weight and wonder it deserves.
Let them call it messy.
Let them call it wild.
Let them say it took too long.
You call it yours.
Call it holy.

Do not shrink to fit into someone else's retelling.
Do not edit yourself to make others comfortable.
Do not hand over your pen
to people who do not know the language of your soul.

You are not a character in someone else's script.
You are the author.
You are the ink.
You are the flame that toasts the leaf and sweetens the cup.

Drink deeply from your own life.
Name every note.
Honor the bitter, exalt the bold, and bless the tender.

Because the woman you are becoming
is not built from perfection—
she is built from presence.
She is forged from truth.
She is sacred because she is

real.

Please let this be your promise:
No matter where the plot twists—
you will not abandon yourself.
You will not erase your name.
You will stand in the center of your story,
and say—
This is me.
And I am enough.
I am more than enough.
And I will never again be spoken for.

Peace and power,

Lorna

LETTER FIFTY THREE

Letter to My Sisters – The Invitation to Rise

I sit in my chair.
The one that has always held me.
And today, in my hands,
I cradle a cup of Wuyi Oolong—
a rich, roasted tea from the cliffs of Fujian.
It is bold and grounding,
a tea that reminds me of the power of returning to self.
Its warmth moves through me like memory,
like truth I've always known.
And as I sip, I think of you.
My sisters.
You have read every word.
You have walked beside me through heartbreak and healing.
You have sat with me in silence,
sipped tea with me in the quiet morning light,
and listened as I laid myself bare.
Now, it is your turn.
It is your turn to rise.
To gather the pieces of yourself
that you tucked away for safekeeping.
To hold your wounds with reverence.
To whisper to your reflection, "You are still worthy."
It is your turn to heal—
not perfectly, not all at once—

but intentionally, gently, truthfully.
To become whole not by erasing your story,
but by honoring every single line of it.
It is your turn to be wild.
To dance barefoot in your own joy.
To love fiercely, without apology.
To stop shrinking.
To stop waiting.
To be.
Never doubt yourself, my sister.
Never doubt the miracle that you are.
The divine breath in your lungs.
The ancient strength in your bones.
You are the daughter of prayers,
the echo of every woman who dared to survive and thrive.
Give yourself grace—
Amazing grace.
Be easy with your becoming.
Be tender with your softness.
Forgive what you could not see then.
Celebrate what you now know.
And love yourself—not just in words,
but in action, in boundaries,
in fierce protection of your light.
But more than anything…
Be the woman that you are.
Be her fully. Be her boldly. Be her now.
And know this—
I am here for you.
Always.

In prayer.
In presence.
In the sisterhood that can never be broken.

With deepest love,

Lorna

LETTER FIFTY FOUR

The Valley and the Mountaintop

Today, I sip some wonderful oolong.
It is warm, toasted, complex—
like memory.
Like the kind of truth that comes slowly,
after the storm has passed.

And as I sit in my chair,
I am reminded:
There are days when the valley wraps around you
like fog.
When the shadows are long,
and your spirit feels small,
and the mountaintop seems like a story
you once believed in but can no longer see.

There are days when you walk alone.
When the silence feels too loud.
When everything good seems far away,
and the ache of waiting becomes its own kind of prayer.

But beloved, don't lose faith.
The valley is not a punishment.
The valley is a place of becoming.
The valley teaches you how to sit with yourself.

How to listen for your own voice

when the world is quiet.
How to find beauty in the smallest things—
a cup of tea,
a soft breeze,
a single step forward.

The valley builds your strength
in ways the mountaintop never could.
It grows your roots.
It steadies your breath.
It reminds you that low does not mean lost.
It reminds you that even here,
even now,
you are still held.

And though you may not feel it yet—
you are moving.
Slowly, quietly, faithfully—
you are rising.

Because you were never meant to stay in the valley.
You were meant to learn from it.
To gather its wisdom.
To carry its quiet strength with you
as you climb.

And you will climb.
One step.

One breath.
One day at a time.

The mountaintop will come again.
The light will return.
The joy will rise to meet you.

But for now,
let your oolong warm your hands.
Let this chair hold your weariness.
And let this truth settle in your bones:

You are not forgotten.
You are not behind.
You are becoming.

The valley is not the end of the story.
It is the sacred beginning.

Lorna

LETTER FIFTY FIVE

You Are Stronger Than You Know

Today, I sit in my chair,
tea in hand,
watching the steam curl like a gentle reminder
that even what rises from heat
can be beautiful.

I breathe.
I settle.
And I write this letter to the part of me
that sometimes forgets her own strength.

There will be days when the path disappears beneath you.
When you question the choices you've made,
when the silence of waiting becomes almost unbearable.
When you wonder if the dream is still yours—
or if it ever was.

But I want you to know this:
You are not weak for having moments of doubt.
You are not failing because you're tired.
You are human.
You are healing.
You are growing stronger in ways you cannot yet see.

Do not mistake stillness for stagnation.
Do not mistake solitude for absence.
Do not mistake heartbreak for defeat.

Everything you've walked through
has been shaping you,
preparing you,
carving out space for the woman you are becoming.

Even now—especially now—
you are being fortified.

And if the tears come, let them.
They are not your enemy.
They are the river washing you clean.
They are your body's way of saying:
We are ready to release what no longer serves us.

So lift your head, gently.
Straighten your spine.
Breathe deeply into your belly.
Place your hand on your heart.
And remember:

You have survived everything that tried to break you.
You have risen after every fall.
You have loved even after loss.
And that kind of woman—
that kind of strength—
is holy.

You are not behind.
You are not alone.
You are not too late.
You are simply in the sacred middle of your becoming.

Keep going, love.
You are stronger than you know.

Lorna

LETTER FIFTY SIX

The Woman Who Thrives

Today, I sit in my chair.

I hold my tea with quiet reverence,
not for the tea itself—
but for the woman I've become while sipping it.
Strong.
Steady.
Unshaken.

There was a time when I only wanted to survive.
To get through the day.
To make it to the next morning with my dignity intact.

But I am no longer in survival.
I am in arrival.
I have stepped into my own power,
and I am no longer afraid of what that means.

Because thriving is not a performance.
It is a posture.
It is how I walk into rooms—
with softness and fire,
with grace and command,
with a spine like steel wrapped in silk.

I thrive because I've done the work.
The deep, soul-wrenching, gut-honest work.
The shedding.
The sitting with pain until it softened in my hands.
The unbecoming of what no longer served me.

And from that soil,
I bloomed.

Not in a rush.
Not all at once.
But in rhythm with my own becoming.

I thrive because I learned to listen to myself—
to honor what I need,
to protect my peace,
to celebrate my joy without shrinking.

I do not apologize for the woman I am now.
I do not explain away my power.
I do not lower my volume to make others feel comfortable.

This is my voice.
This is my life.
This is my season to rise.

To the woman I am today—
you have come so far.
You have earned every bit of the strength you carry.

And you are just getting started.

Walk boldly.
Love freely.
Speak clearly.
Take up your space without hesitation.

You are not just surviving.
You are thriving.

Lorna

LETTER FIFTY SEVEN

How Do You Like Me Now?

A Love Letter to Every Woman Ready to Be Seen

I sip my tea
as I sit in my morning chair—
my place of truth,
my place of reckoning.

Today, the decision sits heavy in my lap,
yet there is a quiet strength brewing within me,
just like the Moroccan mint steeping in my cup—
bold, bright, alive.

I am losing my hair.
Not in shame,
but in surrender.
Most of it—male pattern baldness, they say.
But what I see now
is something far more sacred:
a transformation.

And I don't want to cover it.
Not with wigs, not with pretense,
not with shame.
I want to show the world who I am.

Not edited.
Not concealed.
Not filtered through someone else's idea of beauty.

So, I made the decision.
To shave it all.
To bare my crown.
To walk into this next chapter
bald, bold, and breathtaking.

I thought I would cry.
I thought sadness would hold court.
But it didn't.

Instead, I felt… free.
I felt… strange.
I felt… me.
There was power in that moment the hum of the clippers,
the last strand falling like a past self shedding,
the cool breeze greeting the skin of my head
for the very first time.

And what rose in me wasn't grief,
but sovereignty.
This is me.
All of me.
No more hiding.
No more apologies.
No more shrinking in rooms that demand smallness.

This is me,
in my fullest form.
Unmasked.
Unbothered.
Unstoppable.

And so, I say to the world.
How do you like me now?
This is not brokenness.
This is not loss.
This is arrival.
This is truth,
shining from the top of my head
to the depths of my soul.

And to you yes, you, beloved woman
who sits quietly in the bathroom,
combing thinning strands,
watching the hair fall into the sink
like petals after a storm this is your invitation.

You are not broken.
You are not less.
You are not alone.

To the woman who scrolls through photos
of what once was whispering, I used to be pretty—
darling, you still are.

To the woman who dreads the wind,

terrified it will lift the illusion—
you don't have to live in fear anymore.

Unless you choose to wear the wig,
unless you find joy in it,
then wear it with pride.
But not out of shame.
Not out of silence.
Not because the world said you should.

Because bald is not just beautiful.
Bald is sacred.
Bald is free.
Bald is powerful.

What if your baldness is not the end of something
but the beginning of a becoming?
What if the shedding is the blessing?
Let your scalp feel the air and the sun.
Let your true features be framed
by confidence, not concealment.
Let the world adjust to your truth.

You are not your hair.
You are your light.
You are your courage.
You are your voice,
your grace,
your fire,
your fierce softness.

You carry healing in your veins.
The ancestors whispered it long ago.
You were called before birth,
before fear, before shame ever touched your name.

So, rise.
Bare-headed and glorious.
Walk tall in your temple.
Speak your name into the wind.
Shine, sister.
Shine all the way through.

Because your beauty
has never lived in your hair.
It has always lived
in you.

And the world
has been waiting
to see you just as you are.

Lorna

LETTER FIFTY EIGHT

I Am a Healer

Today the tea I sip is a beautiful Moroccan mint—
refreshing, bold, and alive.

Moroccan mint tea, also known as Atay,
is more than just a drink.
It is a symbol of hospitality, tradition,
and warmth in North African culture.
Made from a blend of Chinese gunpowder green tea
and fresh spearmint leaves,
sweetened generously with sugar,
this tea is typically poured high from a silver pot into small,
delicate glasses—
a ritual that both cools the tea and honors the guest.

As I sip this vibrant infusion,
I feel its coolness awaken something deep within me.
A reminder.
A returning.

Today, I will not dim my light for anyone.
Not for comfort, not for approval, not for belonging.
I will not shrink from my greatness to make others more
comfortable with their smallness.
I will not apologize for my fire.

I will not abandon my calling for anyone.
Because this calling was written in my bones.
It was whispered to my soul
before I ever drew breath.

This work—this healing—
was not a career I stumbled into,
but a birthright I remembered.

It becomes my solemn duty
to make a difference in the world.
To speak truth when silence is easy.
To show up when others hide.
To love fiercely, to serve boldly,
to walk with the wisdom of women who came before me.

I knew even before I was born there was a calling on my life.
I felt it in the womb.
I heard the ancestors humming it
in lullabies only my spirit could hear.

I am a healer.
And I will no longer shrink from that.

I carry medicine in my words,
remedies in my hands,
comfort in my presence.
I am water in a dry land.
I am balm to the weary.

The ancestors gave me this gift,
wrapped it in courage,
sealed it with purpose.

And so, I rise.
And so, I serve.
And so, it is.

Lorna

LETTER FIFTY NINE

Reclaim

I sip tea.
I sit in my favorite chair.
Today, I reclaim the part of me that I abandoned.

The soft, unguarded woman
who once laughed without asking permission.
The girl who dreamed aloud
before the world told her to whisper.

Today, I set boundaries,
not walls—but gates.
Gates that open for love
and close gently to what drains me.

Today, I put forth the best of me
not the polished, not the perfect,
but the true.

That part of me that says,
I am worthy
even when no one claps,
even when the room is silent.

That part of me that is carefree,

who dances barefoot in the kitchen
and sings off-key in the shower.

That part of me that rejoices
when another woman rises,
knowing her light doesn't dim mine—
it reminds me to shine.

That part of me that gives,
not to earn love,
but because love lives in me,
freely, endlessly,
beautifully.

Today, I sip tea.
I return to myself.
And that… is more than enough.

Lorna

LETTER SIXTY

My Why

Today I sit in my chair, and I sip—not tea, but a tisane.
I sip Desert Sage. Simply, simple pleasure.
A cooling blend of peppermint and spearmint.
It wraps around me gently, yet with quiet power.
It is not my usual morning cup,
but today it's exactly what my spirit craved.
Because it takes me back—
to the hills of my childhood in Jamaica,
to early mornings where the scent of mint rose
from the kitchen like prayer in steam.
To a time when women gathered in wisdom,
when herbs healed more than the body.

Today, I sip because I need to reconnect.
Today, I want to speak of my why.

The world sees the what—
the travels, the speaking, the teaching,
the company, the campaigns,
the relentless movement forward.
But it is the why that anchors it all.
The why that beats at the core of every action, every choice.
It is my why that led me to walk among rebels
in the Democratic Republic of the Congo,

to sit beside women whose lives had been torn apart by violence,
to look into eyes that had seen too much and say:
You are seen. You are sacred. I will not turn away.

It is my why that draws me back to Ghana
again and again,
to stand shoulder to shoulder with midwives,
to teach compassionate patient care
not just as a medical protocol,
but as a spiritual calling.
To whisper to the weary: you matter,
and so does the way you serve.

It is my why that birthed Desert Sage,
not just as a lifestyle company,
but as a living circle of healing and purpose.
A space where the sale of tea funds scholarships—
so young women can rise, study, become midwives,
and catch life with their own hands.

Because this is not just about tea.
It is about transformation.
It is about legacy.
It is about rewriting the story
for women who have been told their dreams
are too small,
or their lives expendable.

My why is not a mission statement.
It is a calling.

It is the quiet fire that burns in my chest
when the world is sleeping.
It is the sacred thread that connects
my grandmother's garden in Jamaica
to a birth room in Accra
to a healing circle in Congo
to a kitchen in Coconut Grove.

And so today, I drink deeply.
Not just from my cup, but from the well of purpose.
Because I intend to live this life
unapologetically and fiercely.
Because I remember who I am.
And I remember why.

Lorna

LETTER SIXTY ONE

I Carry the Wisdom of All the Women Before Me

I sip tea in my beautiful chair. The light moves gently across the room, and I feel a sacred stillness settle over me. A knowing. A remembering. I carry the wisdom of all the women before me.

I carry the hush of my grandmother's prayers, whispered into the threads of early morning. I carry the defiance in my mother's voice when she said, No more. I carry the grace of the aunties who made joy from scraps, who turned rice and stories into feasts of resilience.

I carry the rhythm of the women who danced barefoot on red earth, who cooked over open flames, who nursed nations from their breasts and still found the strength to laugh—deep, full-bodied, honest laughter. I may not know all their names. But I know their strength. It lives in my hips, in my heart, in the way I rise again and again when the world tries to unmake me. And when I speak truth—when my voice trembles and I speak it anyway—I know it is not just my voice. It is theirs too. It is every woman who was silenced. Every woman made small. Every woman who dared to dream in secret. I am what they dreamed. I am what they prayed would survive. So, I walk tall. Not in arrogance, but in reverence. When I sit at the table, I bring them with me. When I love, I do so with a tenderness they weren't always given. When I rest, I rest without guilt—because I am the answered prayer of a woman who never had the time.

Let the world feel them in me. Let them know that I have come through the fire, holding stories in my bones, holding medicine in my presence. I don't have to know everything. I just have to remember: I carry the wisdom of all the women before me. And that is more than enough.

Lorna

LETTER SIXTY TWO

I'm Sorry for All the Times I Didn't Choose You

I sip tea in my beautiful chair. The warmth of the cup grounds me, but today, the warmth feels tinged with sorrow—because I need to tell you something I've never said aloud.

I'm sorry. I'm sorry for all the times I didn't choose you. I chose silence instead of speaking your truth. I chose pleasing others over protecting your peace. I chose rooms that didn't see you, people who didn't honor you, and love that asked you to shrink. I looked the other way when you cried in private. I called your needs, too much. I mistook your longing for weakness. I told you to wait. To settle. To be grateful for crumbs. I abandoned you, even while asking the world to accept you.

I see it now—and it breaks my heart. You were never asking for too much. You were asking to be seen. To be safe. To be held in the wholeness of your joy and your pain. Instead of being the one to give that to you, I made you earn it through perfection, through performance, through pretending.

But not anymore. I choose you now. In public and in private. In celebration and in sorrow. In your brilliance and in your breaking. I choose your voice, your softness, your needs. I choose your boundaries, your laughter, your fire. I choose your becoming.

From this day forward, I vow to stop abandoning myself. To stop leaving myself last. To stop negotiating my worth with people who haven't earned my presence. I vow to return. Again, and again. To you. To us. Because no one deserves my loyalty more than the woman who has survived everything—and still dares to love.

I'm sorry for all the times I didn't choose you. But I choose you now. And I will keep choosing you.

Lorna

LETTER SIXTY THREE

I Sit Sipping My Tea, Dancing in the Light

I Sit Sipping My Tea, Dancing in the Light The morning sun filters through the window and falls softly across my skin. There are no alarms blaring, no urgent texts to answer, no pressure to be anything other than what I am. Just me, the warmth of my cup, and this moment—unhurried, unspectacular, and holy.

I used to live in the rush. Running from one expectation to the next. Filling every silence with distraction. Mistaking movement for meaning. Now, I understand the power of stillness. I understand that healing does not always announce itself. Sometimes it arrives like this—on a quiet morning, wrapped in steam and light, asking nothing but that I be present. I breathe deeply. I let my shoulders fall. I let joy find me, not in the grand moments, but in the gentle ones.

There is a version of me that danced only when no one was watching, that laughed too cautiously, that believed softness was weakness. But this woman—this one sipping tea and moving slowly—knows better. She knows that dancing in the light means honoring all the parts of herself. The weary parts. The waiting parts. The wondrous parts. She does not rush her healing. She no longer begs for love that costs her peace. She does not chase belonging—because she already belongs to herself.

At another pace, I have learned to stay. To sit with my thoughts instead of running from them. To listen to my body. To forgive myself for not knowing sooner. To celebrate the smallest acts of grace—making my bed, watering a plant, brewing a perfect cup of tea.

At another pace, I reclaim the sacred ordinary. I write this to remember: I do not have to earn my worth. I do not have to perform my value. I do not have to keep up with a world that never learned how to rest. I am allowed to move slowly. I am allowed to be light. I am allowed to bloom in my own time.

And so, at another pace, I sip, I breathe, I dance. Not for anyone else. Not for approval or applause. But because the light has finally found me, and I am unafraid to live in it.

Lorna

LETTER SIXTY FOUR

You Are Not Behind—You Are Becoming

I sip tea in my beautiful chair. And as the warmth fills me, so does the truth: I am not behind. I am becoming.

I know what it feels like to scroll through other people's lives and wonder if I missed the boat. To hear the ticking of invisible clocks. To watch birthdays come and go with dreams still waiting in the wings. To whisper to myself, I should be further along by now.

But today, I speak back to that lie. I am not late. I am on a path that honors my rhythm, not the world's rush. I am not in competition with anyone else's timeline. I am not a failure because I bloomed differently, because I paused, because I healed first. Becoming is not always visible. It does not announce itself with fanfare or applause.

Sometimes it's quiet—the gentle act of getting out of bed, the sacred "no" whispered in a space where I once said "yes" to please others, the decision to love myself in the absence of external affirmation. And when I doubt, when I ache for progress, when I forget what's unfolding beneath the surface, I remind myself: The seed never questions its darkness. The caterpillar does not shame itself for needing a cocoon. I am allowed to evolve slowly. To rewrite chapters. To rest when I'm tired. To begin again—again and again. There is no perfect pace for becoming. Only presence.

Today, I honor where I am. I honor the soft rebuilding. I honor the spaces I've outgrown and the ones I'm just now growing into. I honor the version of me that held it all together, and the version of me now choosing to come undone in order to live more fully. This is not the middle. This is not the delay. This is the becoming. And it is holy.

I sip tea in my beautiful chair. The steam curls like a prayer, rising into the stillness. And today, my thoughts drift to you. My beloved. I wish you knew me. Not just the version of me you liked best—the easy smile, the laughter, the warmth that wrapped around you when the world turned cold. I wish you knew the me who trembled when I loved too deeply. The me who wanted to be seen not as perfect, but as present. The me who brought my whole heart to the table, hoping you'd meet me there.

I wish you saw me. Not just my beauty or my strength, but the ache I carried when you pulled away. I wish you saw the quiet way I fought for you in silence. I wish you understood the love I wanted to give you—unconditional, unguarded, unafraid. But I know now that wishing doesn't build bridges. And love, real love, does not have to beg to be received.

So, I let you go. Not in bitterness. Not in anger. But in hope. I free you with the prayer that one day, you will return—not out of need, but out of wholeness. Return ready. Ready to love. Ready to be loved. And if you never return, I will still be whole. Because I stayed with myself. I chose me. I honored the love I carried even when it had nowhere to land. This, too, is love. Letting go with tenderness. Holding space without holding on. So go. With grace. And maybe one day, if the stars align and the healing is true, you will return. And this time, we will both be ready.

I sip tea in my beautiful chair. The morning is quiet, but I am not. There is something stirring in me today—something steady, certain, and sacred. My voice is my ministry. For years, I silenced parts of myself to keep the peace. I swallowed the truth when it trembled on my tongue. I made myself smaller so others wouldn't feel uncomfortable in the presence of my knowing. But no more. My voice is not an accident. It is not too much. It is not too loud. It is not unladylike or unbecoming. It carries stories. It carries prayers. It carries justice. It carries healing. When I speak, I speak for the women who were never allowed to raise their voices. The ones who were called angry when they were only honest. The ones who were taught that silence was survival. The ones who were punished for their truth.

But I am not afraid of my truth anymore. I have learned that my voice is not just sound—it is service. It is sanctuary. It is sacred disruption and sacred comfort, both at once. I use my voice to teach, to weep, to rise, to call things by their name. I use my voice to bless. To soothe. To burn down what needs to go and breathe life into what is being born. When I speak, I am not just telling my story. I am restoring something ancient, something holy, something whole.

So today, I do not hide behind modesty or fear. I speak. I speak from the fire and from the ashes. I speak with the softness of compassion and the sharp edge of wisdom. I speak because it is my calling. And I will not mute my ministry for anyone's comfort. This voice—this beautiful, powerful voice— is not just mine. It is a gift. A legacy. A light. And I intend to use it well.

I sip tea in my beautiful chair. And as the cup warms my hands, I think about all the ways I've been taught to be strong. To stand tall. To keep going. To never let them see me cry. To harden myself against disappointment. To tighten my jaw, square my shoulders, and push through. But I know something different now. Softness is strength. To remain tender in a world that demands hardness—that is strength. To feel deeply and still rise, again and again—that is strength. To respond with grace instead of vengeance, with compassion instead of cruelty—that is sacred resilience.

I am not strong because I never break. I am strong because I allow myself to feel. Because I let the tears come. Because I do not shame myself for needing rest, or care, or love. My softness is not a weakness to be hidden. It is a wisdom. A power. A quiet kind of knowing. It is the warmth in my voice, the gentleness in my touch, the way I sit with someone's pain without needing to fix it. There was a time I wore emotional armor just to make it through the day. I confused detachment for protection. I believed I had to be steel to be safe. But now I understand: Steel cannot hold a newborn. Steel cannot comfort a friend. Steel cannot bloom. And I was never meant to be steel. I was meant to be a garden. A river. A balm. A truth-teller with tenderness as my guide.

I am learning to lead with softness. To show up open-hearted, even if I've been hurt. To speak love, even when the world is loud with cruelty. To give myself the softness I so often give to others. I am learning to honor the woman who cries without apology, who loves with abandon, who forgives without forgetting her worth. That woman is not fragile. That woman is powerful beyond measure. Softness is not surrender. It is a choice. A revolutionary one. And I choose it. Every time.

Lorna

LETTER SIXTY FIVE

The Woman I Saw in My Reflection

This morning, the sun pours through my window like grace.

I sit in my chair, the one that has held me through both doubt and revelation.
In my cup is English Breakfast—bold, comforting, ancestral.
A tea that does not flinch from truth.
A tea that reminds me of mornings past,
of women who rose with the dawn
and faced the world without apology.

And I understand now—
perhaps more deeply than ever before—
that everything that has happened in my life
was a mirror, a message, a masterclass.

The good things, the soul-singing joy, the sweet surprises—yes.
But also, the disappointments.
The betrayals.
The heartbreaks I thought I'd never recover from.
The moments I wanted to cast blame, point fingers,
fold into myself.

But to become whole,
I had to stop waiting for someone to come fix it.

I had to stop waiting for the apology that would never arrive,
the closure that would not be mailed.
I had to step out of the story of victimhood,
and into the truth of my own power.

I had to take ultimate responsibility for my life.
Not in shame. Not in guilt.
But in clarity. In courage.
In the sacred act of reclaiming my narrative.

Because when I own it all—every page, every plot twist—
I can also rewrite it.
I can alchemize it.
I can become new.

So, what does it look like to take full responsibility for your life?
Let me show you the roadmap, woman to woman. Tea in hand.
Soul ready.

1. Radical Ownership
Say it out loud: This is my life. Not my mother's, not my ex-lover's, not my boss's.
Mine.
I stop blaming.
I stop outsourcing my power.
I look gently but honestly at the choices
I've made, the patterns I've repeated.
And I say: What am I meant to learn here?

2. Rewriting the Story
Once I own the truth, I get to edit the script.
I can forgive what no longer needs holding.
I can shift my beliefs from "why me" to "what now."
I begin to live from intention, not reaction.
I stop repeating the old scenes expecting a new ending.
I write a new chapter.

3. Taking Inspired Action
Responsibility doesn't mean sitting in shame.
It means getting up every day and doing something
with what I've learned.
I speak differently.
I choose my circle more consciously.
I protect my peace.
I invest in my healing.

And I live from a place of quiet power.
Becoming whole is not about being perfect.
It's about being present.
It's about being honest with yourself.
It's about drinking your tea and whispering:
I will not abandon myself. Not now. Not ever.

And that, dear sister, is the beginning of everything.

With love and a full heart,

Lorna

LETTER SIXTY SIX

And So, I Rise

I sip tea in my beautiful chair. And today, as the last light of this journey touches my skin, I breathe in the fullness of all I have remembered. This has not just been a book. It has been a homecoming. I have gathered the pieces— the strong, the soft, the scarred, the sacred. I have named the wounds and honored the women. I have danced at the water's edge. I have wept for my younger self. I have stood in the reflection of the woman I have become and whispered, Thank you. This is the soul's journey: To shed the armor. To embrace the softness. To walk in the fullness of your name. To remember that you are not behind— you are becoming.

Each letter has been a mirror. Each story, a prayer. Each page, a place to lay down the burden and rise with new breath. I carry the wisdom of all the women before me. I am the prayer of my ancestors. I walk with the fire of Nanny, the strength of Esther, the vision of Wangari, and the stillness of the women who gathered under moonlight and mango trees. I am not here by chance. I am here on purpose. For a time such as this.

And now, I rise. With every scar. With every triumph. With every truth I once thought I had to hide. I rise not just for me, but for the women watching, for the daughters dreaming, for the generations yet to be born who will one day read these pages and know that wholeness is not a destination—it is a returning. You do not need to be perfect to be powerful. You do not need to be loud to be worthy. You only need to be true.

Werever you are, if your voice shakes, speak anyway. If your hands tremble, write anyway. If your heart is healing, love anyway. Let the soft life find you. Let sisterhood hold you. Let God meet you in the quiet. Let destiny walk with you—step by step. You are becoming whole. And that is the most beautiful thing you will ever do.

Affirmation – I Am Aligned With Wholeness
Today, I sit in my chair.
I pause.
I look at my tea—
the liqueur is warm, golden, steady.
I watch the steam rise like prayer.
I close my eyes.
I breathe.
In this moment, I remember:
I am whole.
Not because everything is perfect,
but because I choose presence over pressure,
grace over grind,
truth over illusion.
With every sip, I nourish not just my body,
but my spirit.
I release chaos.
I welcome clarity.
I align with the divine rhythm of my life.

I am not rushing.
I am not chasing.
I am rooted.
I am rising.
I am worthy of stillness,
of softness,
of sacred care.
This moment is enough.
I am enough.
I am becoming whole.

Affirmation – I Am Held And Whole
Today, I sit in my chair.
I hold my tea in both hands—
the warmth steadies me.
I breathe in stillness,
and I let it rise through me like light.
I remind myself:
I am not alone.
I am not broken.
I am held—by the universe,
by grace,
by my own becoming.
I bless the love that was.
I grieve it with gentleness,
with gratitude,
with grace.
It shaped me, but it does not define me.
I release fear.
I release doubt.

I release the old stories
that asked me to question my strength.
I do not carry them anymore.
I trust the quiet wisdom inside me.
I trust the peace that follows truth.
I am at peace.
All is well.

Lorna

LETTER SIXTY SEVEN

Today I Sit in My Chair with English Breakfast

A Letter on Radical Responsibility

This morning, the sun pours through my window like grace.

I sit in my chair, the one that has held me through both doubt and revelation.
In my cup is English Breakfast—bold, comforting, ancestral.
A tea that does not flinch from truth.
A tea that reminds me of mornings past,
of women who rose with the dawn
and faced the world without apology.

And I understand now—
perhaps more deeply than ever before—
that everything that has happened in my life
was a mirror, a message, a masterclass.

The good things, the soul-singing joy, the sweet surprises—yes.
But also, the disappointments.
The betrayals.
The heartbreaks I thought I'd never recover from.
The moments I wanted to cast blame, point fingers,
fold into myself.
But to become whole,
I had to stop waiting for someone to come fix it.

I had to stop waiting for the apology that would never arrive,
the closure that would not be mailed.
I had to step out of the story of victimhood,
and into the truth of my own power.

I had to take ultimate responsibility for my life.
Not in shame. Not in guilt.
But in clarity. In courage.
In the sacred act of reclaiming my narrative.

Because when I own it all—every page, every plot twist—
I can also rewrite it.
I can alchemize it.
I can become new.

So, what does it look like to take full responsibility for your life?
Let me show you the roadmap, woman to woman. Tea in hand.
Soul ready.

1. Radical Ownership
Say it out loud: This is my life. Not my mother's, not my ex-lover's, not my boss's.
Mine.
I stop blaming.
I stop outsourcing my power.
I look gently but honestly at the choices
I've made, the patterns I've repeated.

And I say: What am I meant to learn here?

2. Rewriting the Story
Once I own the truth, I get to edit the script.
I can forgive what no longer needs holding.
I can shift my beliefs from "why me" to "what now."
I begin to live from intention, not reaction.
I stop repeating the old scenes expecting a new ending.
I write a new chapter.

3. Taking Inspired Action
Responsibility doesn't mean sitting in shame.
It means getting up every day and doing something
with what I've learned. I speak differently.
I choose my circle more consciously.

I protect my peace.
I invest in my healing.
And I live from a place of quiet power.
Becoming whole is not about being perfect.
It's about being present.
It's about being honest with yourself.
It's about drinking your tea and whispering:
I will not abandon myself. Not now. Not ever.

And that, dear sister, is the beginning of everything.

With love and a full heart,

Lorna

LETTER SIXTY EIGHT

Today I Sit in My Chair with Determination and Tea

A Roadmap to Becoming Whole After Love and Loss

This morning, I sip my tea slowly.
A deep, malty English Breakfast once again—
strong, steady, the kind of tea that wraps its arms around you
and whispers, "You can do this."

I sit in my beautiful chair, the one that has held me
in every version of myself—
the hopeful woman in love,
the woman undone by heartbreak,
and now…
the woman who is ready.

Today I am pondering.
Today I am strategizing.
I am ready to do the hard work.
Not the performative kind—
but the sacred work of rebuilding, restoring,
e-rooting myself.

I have loved. And I have lost.
And for a while, I thought I might stay in the ache of it forever.

But now, I choose something different.
Now, I choose me.

And so I ask the question:
What does it look like to become whole again?
What does it take to rise after your heart has been broken open?
Here is what I've come to know.
Here is the roadmap I followed and offer to you.

1. Feel It All

Don't rush past the grief.

Don't bury the memories.

Let the pain have its voice—but not the microphone forever.

Feel the tenderness, the longing, the absence.

Cry in the shower. Journal in the dark.

Let yourself feel, so you can truly heal.

2. Rewrite the Inner Narrative

Watch your thoughts.

The ones that whisper, "You were not enough."

The ones that scream, "You will never love like that again."

Catch them, question them, replace them.

Tell a new story:

"I am enough. I am worthy. I am still becoming."

3. Rebuild Your Rituals

Make tea in the morning with reverence.

Light candles.

Speak affirmations into the mirror.

Take long walks.

Dance barefoot.

Create a rhythm that honors your soul's recovery.

Your life is not broken—it's being reimagined.

4. Choose Your Circle With Care

Surround yourself with people who don't rush your process.

People who remind you who you are when you forget.

People who sit beside you, not above you.

People who say, "Let's rise, together."

Not all relationships are meant to last—

but healing friendships are meant to begin.

5. Invest in Your Becoming

Therapy. Coaching. Books. Retreats.

Whatever you need to come home to yourself.

Pour energy into the version of you you're building.

Not for revenge. Not to prove anything.

But because you are deserving of your own devotion.

6. Love Again—But Start with You

Let love find you again, if it will.

But make sure you've first fallen in love with yourself.

Love your mind. Love your skin. Love your solitude.

Learn what brings you joy.

Become so full that any new love is a bonus, not a rescue.

This is not a straight path.

There will be days when you fall back,

when you ache, when you question if you've made progress at all.

But keep going, dear woman.

Keep sitting in your chair.

Keep sipping your tea.

Keep choosing yourself.

Because wholeness is not a destination.

It is a daily devotion.

And you, my sister, are worth the work.

With quiet strength and love,

Lorna

LETTER SIXTY NINE

The Mirror Doesn't Lie.

A Letter to the Woman I Am Becoming

Today, I came to my favorite chair.
Tea in one hand.
Mirror in the other.
Because today, I needed to see myself clearly.
Not the version I soften for others.
Not the version that performs.
Just me.
Face to face.
Eye to eye.
Heart to soul.

Because the truth is—
the mirror doesn't lie.

Mirror work is sacred.
It is emotional.
It is psychological.
It is spiritual.
It is looking into your own eyes

and saying the things no one else dares to say.
It is not about vanity.
It is about intimacy—with the self.
It's how I come back to me.

So today, I looked.
And I spoke.
And I wept.

Because I had something I needed to say to myself.

I flashed back through the relationship.
The highs. The hopes. The hush of red flags
I didn't want to hear.
And as I searched my own eyes in the glass,
two truths stood still before me:

One, he does not love me. He never did.
Two, he is not capable—or ready—to give me or anyone the kind of love I need.

And the truth is… either one could be right.
Or both.
But whichever one it is—the result is the same.
And my heart feels it all the same.

So I turned from hope to evidence.
I looked at behavior.
Because behavior is the real mirror.

A person who loves you doesn't disappear.
They don't forget your birthday.
They don't go silent on Christmas.
They don't let New Year's Eve pass without reaching out.
No. A person who loves you wants to be the first voice
you hear in the morning
and the last whisper before you sleep.
Even if they're oceans away.
Even if it's just for a moment.
Love makes time.
Not excuses.

A person who loves you thinks about you.
They choose things for you with care.
They show up for joy, for sorrow, for celebration.
They don't treat you like an afterthought.
You are not a burden to them.
You are a joy spot.

And when those things are missing—
when connection is a chore,
when presence is absent,

when thoughtfulness is nowhere to be found—
you know.
You know what's true.

As the old saying goes:
"They're just not that into you."
And that's okay.

It's going to hurt.
Yes, it will feel like breaking.
Yes, there will be tears.
But oh, beloved—
what a beautiful, freeing experience it is
when you finally accept it.
When you finally stop waiting for the apology,
the change, the chase.
When you gather your truth and move on.

Today, I looked in the mirror.
And I didn't flinch.
Because what I saw was a woman rising.
A woman healing.
A woman no longer willing to shrink
for someone who never saw her in full light.

I looked in the mirror.

And I saw love.
My own.

With grace,
The Woman I Am Becoming,

Lorna

LETTER SEVENTY

The Most Important Decision

Today, I sit in my favorite chair.
The one that knows the curve of my back and the weight of my prayers.
And in my cup is something warm—gentle, grounding.
This is my reflection time.
A quiet reckoning.
Because I've heard it many times—
and now I believe it with every thread of my becoming:
The most important decision
you will ever make in your life
is who you choose as your partner.

Not where you work.
Not what house you buy.
Not even what dreams you chase.
Because whoever you choose to share your life with
will either anchor your peace or disturb your soul.

They will either make you strong or make you weak.
They will stretch your days with laughter and life—
or shorten your breath with stress and silence.
This decision affects your longevity.
It affects your health.
It shapes the quality of your everyday living.

It can lift your spirit or crush your joy.

This person holds the power to build you up
or break you down.
To pour into you or drain you dry.
To nourish your becoming
or constantly make you question it.

So, let's speak truth.

Love is not enough.
Chemistry fades. Butterflies lie.
You need someone whose presence feels like peace.
Not performance. Not pressure.
Just peace.
Choose someone who listens—not just with ears,
but with the heart.
Someone who doesn't just tolerate your strength,
but celebrates it.
Who sees your scars and calls them sacred,
not shameful.

Choose someone who prays for you when you don't have words.
Who knows the language of your silence.
Someone who doesn't vanish when life gets hard,
but leans in with gentleness and grace.

Choose someone who doesn't make you question your worth.
You are not meant to convince someone to choose you.
Real love never has to be begged for.

You will not have to shrink.
You will not have to carry the whole thing on your back.

Choose someone who chooses you back—
every single day.
Someone whose actions match their words,
whose presence calms your nervous system,
whose laughter fills the room like music.

Because this decision—this sacred choosing—
will shape the way you heal, the way you grow,
the way you mother, if you choose,
the way you sleep at night.
This decision will either water your garden
or scorch your roots.

And let me tell you what I know now:
It's better to be single and whole
than partnered and empty.
It's better to sleep alone in peace
than lie next to someone and feel like you don't exist.

So wait.
Wait for the one who respects your boundaries.
Wait for the one who isn't intimidated by your light.
Wait for the one who doesn't ghost when it gets real.
Wait for the one who wants to grow with you,
not compete with you.
Wait for the one who sees partnership not as ownership,
but as sacred companionship.

And while you wait—
build a life that makes you proud.
Fill it with ritual, with friendships, with laughter, with truth.
Fall in love with yourself.
Be the kind of woman who doesn't need a partner—
but knows she deserves a divine one.

Because you do.

You deserve someone who holds your dreams in their palms
like crystal.
Who cheers for you louder than anyone else.
Who sees your magic and never wants to dim it.
Who shows up when the storms come,
and stays until the rainbow.
Who makes you feel safe, seen, desired, and heard.
And if you've chosen wrong before—grace.
Forgive yourself.
You made that choice with knowledge
you had at the time.
Maybe it was for survival.
Maybe it was for safety.
Maybe it was for comfort, for family, for legacy,
for pragmatism.
Maybe it made sense then.

But now you know better.
Now you choose with wisdom,
with intention, with sacred clarity.

Because this is the most important decision
you will ever make.
Let it be holy.
Let it be honest.
Let it be worthy of the woman you are becoming.
With all my heart,
The Woman I Am Becoming,

Lorna

LETTER SEVENTY ONE

Letter to Self – Choose Your Peace.

My Beloved Self,

Peace and blessings to you today.
I feel the sun in my spirit as I sit in my chair,
hands wrapped around a cup of white tea from Nepal.

The steam curls upward,
and with each breath,
I feel lighter, stronger, clearer.
And this is the truth I need you to hold:
Stop telling people how to treat you.
If they truly cared, they would know.
If you mattered in their heart,
they would not need a manual on how to love you.
They would not need constant reminders
of what makes you feel seen.
I know it is tempting to keep hoping,
to keep giving the benefit of the doubt,
to keep thinking, maybe if I explain one more time,
they will understand.
But your soul is tired of begging for the bare minimum.
Love should not have to be chased.
Respect should not have to be demanded.
You should never have to perform or plead

to be honored by someone who claims to care for you.
If they wanted to, they would.

Let go.
Release the ones who cannot see your worth.
Walk away from the ones who make you feel like a footnote
in their story
instead of the woman you are—
a woman worthy of being the whole chapter.
This is your season to choose your peace.
This is your season to sip your tea in the sunlight
and let your heart expand in freedom.
Do not look back.
Do not chase.
Do not keep giving chances to those
who have already shown you that you are not a priority.
Because life is waiting to give you better.
Love is waiting to meet you where you are—
fully, freely, without condition.
So, protect your peace, my beloved self.
Let the ones who cannot honor you fall away like autumn leaves.
And keep walking into your joy,
head high,
heart open,
whole and free.
With love and resolve,

Me,

Lorna

LETTER SEVENTY TWO

What It Means to Become Whole.

This is a lifelong practice rooted in courage, curiosity, and compassion. Here are some tangible ways to deepen this journey:

1. Integration of the Self:

You stop disowning or denying parts of yourself. This includes unresolved emotions, regrets, flaws, fears, and even past mistakes. Instead of compartmentalizing, you recognize these as parts of your story that inform your resilience and wisdom.

2. Living Authentically:

Wholeness means aligning your inner values with your outer actions. You no longer live to meet others' expectations but strive to live in truth with who you are.

3. Peace with Imperfection:

You accept that being human means being imperfect. Wholeness honors the messiness of life rather than resisting it.

Lorna

LETTER SEVENTY THREE

Embracing Self-Acceptance and Growth

Embracing Self-Acceptance and Growth This is a lifelong practice rooted in courage, curiosity, and compassion. Here are some tangible ways to begin or deepen this journey:

1. Practice Radical Self-Honesty

Ask: What am I not willing to face about myself right now? Be kind—but truthful—with what comes up. Honesty is the first step to growth.

2. Meet Yourself with Compassion

When you stumble, treat yourself like you would a beloved friend. Growth happens when you're safe enough to be vulnerable—not punished for being imperfect.

3. Learn from the Shadow

Explore the parts of you that you hide, repress, or deny (what Jung called the 'shadow'). These often hold keys to your creativity, power, and healing.

4. Commit to Inner Work

Journaling, therapy, meditation, creative expression, and reading—these are tools that help you hear yourself more clearly and grow consciously.

5. Set Boundaries and Say No

Self-acceptance means recognizing what is right for you and having the courage to uphold it, even when it's hard.

6. Embrace Change, Gently

Growth is not linear. It has regressions, breakthroughs, and plateaus. Trust the process, even when it's slow or uncertain. Becoming whole is not about 'fixing' yourself. It's about returning to yourself—again and again—with love, clarity, and a willingness to evolve. Growth isn't about becoming someone else; it's about becoming more you.

Lorna

LETTER SEVENTY FOUR

A Journey into Self-Acceptance and Growth

This morning, I sit quietly in my chair, the one that has always known how to hold me. In my cup, a steaming brew of golden oolong — floral, warm, like a whispered promise. I sip slowly, inviting the stillness. I am not rushing today. I am here to gather myself.

To truly become whole is to embrace the full spectrum of who you are — your light and shadow, strengths and flaws, past and present — with honesty, compassion, and courage. Wholeness isn't perfection or the absence of pain; it's integration. It means no longer disowning parts of yourself to fit an ideal, but instead recognizing that every experience, emotion, and aspect of your being belongs.

Here's how one can embrace the process of self-acceptance and growth:

1. Face Your Shadow
You can't become whole without looking at the parts of yourself you might rather ignore — fear, anger, shame, regret. Carl Jung doesn't mean you're always successful, but it means you're honest called this the "shadow," and he believed we grow when we acknowledge and work with it, not suppress it.

Practice: Journal honestly. Enter the cave you fear. Do shadow work or speak truth in therapy. Let what has been hidden breathe.

2. Be Compassionate Toward Yourself

Self-acceptance begins with self-compassion. Speak to yourself like someone you love. Growth is messy. You will contradict yourself. You will fail. That's part of it.

Practice:

When you notice self-judgment, pause. Place your hand over your heart. Ask, "What would I say to a dear friend in this moment?"

3. Get Curious, Not Critical

Growth comes from inquiry, not condemnation. When something triggers you, instead of reacting, ask why. When you fall into a pattern, ask where it began. Awareness gives you choice.

Practice:

Meditate. Reflect. Ask gently, "What's the lesson here?" instead of "What's wrong with me?"

4. Live with Integrity

Wholeness means aligning your actions with your values. That about the gaps and willing to work on them. And the good news? You don't have to be fixed to be worthy. You're already enough. Already complete in your becoming. With love,

Lorna

AFFIRMATIONS
FROM BECOMING WHOLE

Affirmation One: Morning Light
I rise with grace.

Today, I choose peace.
Today, I honor the woman I am becoming.
I am not behind. I am not broken.
I am exactly where I need to be.
The sun rises for me too.
Favor is finding me now.
I am worthy of rest, of joy, of divine unfolding.

Affirmation Two: Sacred Worth
I am enough, exactly as I am.

I do not chase love.
I do not beg for belonging.
I stand in the fullness of who I am—
soft and strong, gentle and powerful.
I am not waiting to be chosen.
I choose myself.
I am whole.

Affirmation Three: Becoming Bold
I walk in my truth.

Every step I take is sacred.
Even when I am afraid, I move forward.
Even when I stumble, I rise again.

I am becoming bold in the way I love,
in the way I speak,
in the way I show up for my life.
This is my time.
This is my becoming.

MEDITATIONS
FROM BECOMING WHOLE

Meditation One: A Morning Centering
Return to your breath. Return to yourself.

Close your eyes.
Feel the chair beneath you.
Feel your feet on the ground.
Let your shoulders fall, your jaw soften.
Take a slow, deep breath in through your nose...
Hold it gently...
Exhale slowly through your mouth.

Say softly,
I am here.
I am safe.
I am whole.

Let the morning light find your face.
Let it kiss your skin and awaken your spirit.
You do not have to strive today.
You do not have to prove or perform.
You are already enough.
Already beloved.
Already becoming.

Take one more deep breath.
And as you open your eyes,

walk forward with grace.

Meditation Two: A Night of Release
Lay it all down now. The day has done enough.

Close your eyes.
Place your hand on your heart.
Feel its rhythm.
Feel its faithfulness.
Breathe in. Breathe out.

Say gently,
I release this day.
I release the worry, the wondering, the weight.
I did what I could.
I let the rest go.

Breathe again.
Let your belly rise. Let your spirit soften.

You are not alone.
You are not forgotten.
You are held—in love, in grace, in divine care.

Say,
I am worthy of rest.
I am open to healing.
I trust the dark to make way for the dawn.
Sleep, beloved.
Let God do the work while you rest.

LETTER SEVENTY FIVE

How to Become a Woman

A Soul Guide for Rebuilding After Love Lost

Step 1: Sit with the Ruins

First, sit still
Don't rush to clean up the mess.
Let yourself feel what's broken.
Grieve what didn't last.
Grieve the dream, not just the person.
You can't rebuild a life if you deny the ashes.
Sit. Sip tea. Weep if you must.
You are not weak—you are sacred in your sorrow.

Step 2: Tell Yourself the Truth

Whisper it. Write it.
Say what happened out loud:
"I was not loved the way I needed."
"He chose someone else."
"She broke my heart."
Truth will unclog your spirit.

Truth will begin your healing.

This is where you start taking your power back.

Step 3: Reclaim the Mirror

Look at yourself.

Look at her.

The woman who survived.

The one who loved deeply.

The one who now chooses herself.

Say: "I am still worthy."

Say it until your bones believe it.

Step 4: Stop Romanticizing the Past

Do not make a museum of your pain.

Do not turn every sweet memory into a shrine.

Yes, you had good times.

But remember the nights you cried.

The unanswered texts.

The times you felt invisible beside them.

Stop editing the truth to make it prettier than it was.

You deserve better than what hurt you.

Step 5: Clean the Space, Clear the Spirit

Take down the photos.
Wash the sheets.
Throw away the candle you lit for both of you.
Declutter the emotional corners.
Make room for the new.
And as you do, speak this blessing over your home:
"I release what no longer belongs to me."

Step 6: Choose the Work of Wholeness

Healing is not a passive act.
It is daily, gritty, and divine.
Start walking again.
Start drinking water again.
Start reading poetry again.
Start talking to God again.
Begin where you are.
You don't need a 5-year plan.
You just need a willingness to show up for your own life.

Step 7: Call Back Your Power

From every place you gave it away—
Call it back.
From the nights you stayed up hoping.
From the places where you kept shrinking.
From the silence you kept when you should have spoken.
Say: "I want all of me back."
And then stand up.

Step 8: Fall in Love with Yourself Again

Take yourself to dinner.
Dance in your kitchen.
Write letters to your future.
Put on the red lipstick.
Tell yourself:
"I deserve softness.
I deserve pleasure.
I deserve joy that doesn't come with conditions."

Step 9: Open Your Heart Again—But Wiser

Do not close your heart.
Just guard it with truth.
Let love find you again—this time, pure.
This time, mutual.
This time, without sacrifice of self.
You don't need someone to fix you.
You need someone who honors the work you've already done.

Step 10: Keep Becoming

You don't arrive.
You keep unfolding.
Like seasons. Like tea leaves in warm water.
Keep choosing your healing.
Keep choosing your joy.
Keep becoming the woman you promised yourself you'd be.

Lorna

LETTER SEVENTY SIX

Ritual Matters

As I sit in my chair—
the one that has caught every version of my sigh—
I sip my tea slowly.
It is the same each morning.
A cup. A pause. A return.

This is not about the flavor.
It is not about the type of leaf or the color of the steep.
It is about the ritual.
The stillness before the noise.
The choosing of me before I go out to choose the world.

Every day in this season of my life,
I return to this simple rhythm:
chair, cup, breath, me.
And in this quiet act,
I remind myself that I matter.
That care does not have to be grand or loud
to be powerful.
It just has to be consistent.

This cup is a kind of prayer.
It is how I come home to myself.
Before emails. Before decisions. Before demands.

I sit. I sip. I tend to the sacred garden of my being.

And so I say to the woman becoming—
create a ritual that holds you.
It doesn't have to be complicated.
It just needs to be yours.

Maybe it's tea.
Maybe it's journaling at dawn.
Maybe it's walking barefoot in the grass
or lighting a candle at sunset.
But whatever it is—make it a ceremony.
Make it a vow to yourself.
Because ritual matters.
Ritual is remembering.

And self-care is not indulgent.
It is not selfish.
It is survival with grace.
It is the slow healing of what the world forgets to tend.
It is how we gather the scattered parts of us
and bring them back home.

So keep showing up for yourself.
Pour the tea.
Sit in the chair.
Touch your own heart with tenderness.
Because every woman becoming needs a rhythm—

a ritual that reminds her that she is already whole.
With love,

Lorna

LETTER SEVENTY SEVEN

Dear Heart – A Letter on Healing

Dear Heart,
I want to talk to you about healing.
Not the kind of healing that happens in a day,
or with a single deep breath,
or after one long cry.
I mean the kind of healing that takes time.
The kind that moves like a tide—forward and back,
but always moving, always shaping something new in you.

Healing from love…
healing from the ache of emotional trauma…
is a tender, deliberate journey.
It doesn't happen all at once.
It doesn't move in a straight line.

There will be days you feel light again.
Days you wake up and laugh and think,
I am healed. I am whole.
And then, without warning, a memory will brush against you,
a word, a song, a fragrance—
and your heart will stumble.
The ache will rise.

And you may think, I am back at the beginning.
But please, believe me:
You are not back at the beginning.
This is just how healing works.
It tests, it circles, it softens slowly.
Every step you take forward,
every tear that falls and dries,
is proof that you are mending
in ways you cannot yet see.
Your only job is this:

Do not give up.
Do not lose hope.
Take it one day at a time.
Put one foot in front of the other.
Hold your own hand when no one else can.
Yes, the road will be bumpy.
Yes, there will be moments you question if the pain will ever end.
But if you keep going, if you keep choosing yourself,
the result will be beautiful.
I know, because I have walked this road.
I have been bent by heartbreak and made hollow by grief.
I have woken in the night thinking the ache would swallow me.
And yet, here I am—
smiling again,
laughing again,
loving myself again.
Your healing is worth it.
Every quiet moment of care you give yourself is worth it.
Every time you rise, even when your heart is heavy,

is worth it.
So, take your time.
Sip your tea slowly.
Wrap yourself in the soft knowing that you are not broken.
You are becoming.
And the woman you are becoming
is waiting on the other side of this journey,
arms open, heart free,
already proud of you.

With love and understanding,

Me,

Lorna

LETTER SEVENTY EIGHT

Morning Reverie: A Letter to the Woman I Am

This morning, I sit in my chair—the chair that knows me,
that loves me,
the chair that has held my dreams and my tears,
and I cradle my tea in both hands.
The steam rises like a soft whisper,
and I exhale into the quiet.

It is beautiful here.
It is soulful.
This is my morning reverie.
And as I sip, I remember this truth:
I was not put on this earth for myself alone.

The song drifts into my heart—
We Are the World.
I hear it as if the ancestors themselves are singing,
reminding me that we belong to one another,
that the beating of my heart
is tied to the heartbeat of the world.
We are threads in one great tapestry,
and when one life is lost,
the fabric trembles.

I think of the mothers.

Every 90 seconds,
somewhere in the world,

a woman dies from complications of pregnancy—
complications that could have been prevented.
She is somebody's daughter,
somebody's beloved, and she dies
bringing life into the world
Most of these women live in sub-Saharan Africa.
In have walked their villages,
felt the dust rise beneath my feet,
looked into their eyes and seen strength wrapped in fatigue.
I have felt their love for their babies,
their hope that someone, somewhere,
will care enough to make a difference.

This is why I rise from my chair.
This is why my tea becomes my prayer.

I give scholarships to young women in Ghana
to become midwives,
because midwives are the guardians of life.
They stand between heaven and earth,
catching our future in their hands.

And now, mothers across Ghana
drink what the midwives call Mama Lorna's Blessing—
a simple, sacred brew of turkey berry, pineapple, and orange.
It is a gift of love,
a quiet lifeline for mothers with low hemoglobin.

I pay for it myself because service is not charity.
It is love made visible.

I have learned this:
When you become a woman of worth,
when you finally rise into the truth of who you are,
the universe calls you higher.
Life is no longer small.
Your purpose begins to stretch beyond your own walls.
You begin to hear the whisper:
"Give more. Heal more. Love more."

And so today, I walk into my purpose fully.
I hear God's voice.
I hear the ancestors.
I hear the world itself saying,
"Welcome. Welcome home, my daughter.
We have been waiting for your greatness to be revealed."

If you are reading this, my sister,
know this:
The world is waiting for you, too.
Somewhere, a life is waiting for your yes.
Somewhere, your light is needed.
And when you step into that light,
when you become the woman
you were always meant to be,
the universe will rise to meet you,

and the world will whisper,
"Welcome home."

Love,

Lorna

LETTER SEVENTY NINE

Becoming Woman: The Quiet Arrival

My Beloved Self,

Today, I sit in my favorite chair—the one that has held every version of me, from the trembling girl to the woman who now remembers her own name. In my cup is Silver Needle tea, light as morning breath, harvested from the foothills of Kilimanjaro, kissed by mist and carried here as if by grace. I lift it slowly, reverently, for I know this moment is sacred.

I have walked through fire.
I have sat with my pain and named it.
I have traced every scar and whispered,
You are allowed to be here.
I have done the hard work, the quiet work, the soul work.

I have meditated until my thoughts softened into stillness.
I have prayed until my heart felt light in my chest.
I have taken long walks beneath an endless sky,
letting the wind carry away my grief
and the earth cradle my weary steps.

And now… I am home.
Not in a house, or a city, or a country.
Home in myself.

I have stitched myself back together with golden thread.
I have made peace with the mirror.
The woman looking back at me is no longer searching.
She is resting. She is whole. She is happy.

I do not bend to fit love anymore.
I do not bargain to be chosen.
I do not hustle for my worth.
I simply am.

I have gathered the younger me—
the girl who thought she had to be sharp to survive,
who doubted her softness—and I have held her close.
I thank her for her courage. I honor her fight.
But I do not let her drive my life anymore.

I have forgiven.
Others, yes—but mostly myself.
I released the weight of old love,
the unfinished stories, the questions with no answers.
I let them become steppingstones that led me here.
Every ending became an offering,
every goodbye, a blessing in disguise.

And love—oh, love will come.
Not to rescue me. Not to fill me.
But to meet me where I already live:
Full. Rooted. Enough.

Peace has finally found her seat beside me.

Or maybe she was always here, waiting
for me to be still long enough to notice.

This tea, this chair, this breath—they are my altar.
They are the ceremony of my becoming.

I have become woman.
Not by age, not by name, but by the holy act of gathering
every lost piece of myself and saying, Welcome home.
This may be the final letter,
but it is only the beginning—
of walking in the world as I am:
Radiant. Rooted. Ready. Happy.

Let love find me.
Let peace stay with me.
Let my name rise with the morning light.

Because I am no longer waiting.
I am already here.
I am whole.
I am woman.
I am home.

With all the love I once searched for,

Me,

Lorna

LETTER EIGHTY

Losing Ceremony – Welcome Home to Yourself

Losing Ceremony – Welcome Home to Yourself Before you close this book, pause. Breathe in. Breathe out. Feel your own heartbeat—steady, alive, present. You have walked beside me through these pages, through letters of longing, healing, and becoming. Now it is your turn to arrive. This is your moment. To release the weight you've been carrying. To forgive yourself for the times you doubted your worth. To whisper to the mirror, I am enough. Let this be your quiet ceremony:

- Brew a cup of your favorite tea.
- Sit in your sacred space—your "favorite chair," or any place that feels like home.
- Close your eyes and feel the warmth of the cup in your hands.
- Breathe deeply.
- When you are ready, speak your own name out loud.

Say to yourself: I am radiant. I am rooted. I am ready. I am happy. I am whole.

Lorna

Reflection For Your Journal

1. Who am I now that I have arrived at myself?
2. What am I ready to release so that peace can fully stay?
3. What does "home in myself" feel like today?
4. What blessings am I ready to receive with open hands and an open heart?

Write freely. Write honestly. Write as if your soul is listening—because it is.

Welcome home, beautiful one.
This is not the end.
This the beginning of walking the world as fully you.

Love,

Lorna

Becoming Whole Teas

My Dear Sisters,

I have been pouring my heart and soul into something special for you. As I wrote in the pages of Becoming Whole, I dreamed of creating a companion for your quiet moments—a cup to cradle as you read, reflect, and step into your own becoming.

After much care, I am overjoyed to share two beautiful teas crafted just for this journey.

The First

is a delicate oolong, softly floral and serene, a whisper of calm that invites you to pause and breathe.

The Second

is a vibrant berry blend, alive with echinacea, black and red currant, and hibiscus, a joyful cup that feels like laughter and sunshine in your hands.

These are more than teas; they are an offering from my heart to yours—a gentle ritual for the woman you are and the woman you are becoming.

I am so proud to bring these blends to life for our Becoming Whole circle. May each sip remind you that you are worthy of beauty, rest, and moments that belong only to you.

With love,

Lorna

A Day in the Life of My Dream

I woke to the soft hum of the sea this morning. It was the kind of sound that belongs to a lullaby, rhythmic and endless. Even before I opened my eyes, I felt the warmth of Jamaica in my

bones—the sun just beginning its golden stretch across the sky, and the faintest perfume of mango blossoms drifting in through the open shutters of my bedroom.

I sat up in my familiar white bed, the sheets cool against my skin, and wrapped myself in my favorite soft robe—the one that makes me feel like the morning belongs only to me. The house itself seemed to greet me. My white Victorian home by the sea feels alive, as if she too, wakes with the sun, smiling as the light spills across her polished wooden floors.

I padded barefoot to the veranda, my sacred circle of sky and sea. My chair was waiting for me, the one that loves me and holds me like an old friend. I sank into it and closed my eyes, breathing in my island. The breeze carried salt and sun-warmed hibiscus. On the small table beside me, my tea was already waiting: The Water's Edge, a gentle green and white tea from Desert Sage. Steam rose like an offering to the morning sky. I sipped slowly, letting the flavor carry me—grassy, tender, with whispers of sweetness. My soul exhaled.

He came to me then—my beloved. Barefoot and unhurried, his voice still heavy with sleep but soft with love. "Good morning," he said, and the words wrapped around me like music. He kissed me lightly on the lips, and we walked together to the breakfast table set on the veranda.

Our chef had prepared a feast, though it felt more like a poem. Coconut croissants still warm from the oven, papaya slices glistening with dew, pineapples and mangoes cut like little suns, and fresh orange juice that still smelled of the grove by the side of the house. We laughed softly over breakfast, our words floating into the morning air. We live like this—without hurry, without noise, surrounded by nature and love.

After breakfast, we walked through the garden. Everything we need grows here—mangoes, bananas, papayas, grapefruit, limes. The herbs thrive in their little beds: thyme, lemongrass, basil, and mint, still cool from the night. I picked a sprig of mint and rubbed it between my fingers, releasing its bright scent into the world.

By midday, we strolled down the path to the water. Our home rests on a small cliff, and the walk down is a dance between shade and sunlight. Bougainvillea trails down the rocks like pink fire, and the sea greets us with soft, clear waves. We swam in the warmth of the Caribbean, the water holding us the way the island always has, gently and without judgment.

Afternoon was for rest and joy. We read books on the veranda, listened to music—soft jazz and the occasional reggae note carried from a neighbor's home down the coast. The chef brought us a colorful vegetarian lunch: roasted breadfruit, callaloo, and a salad of fresh mango, avocado, and lime. Every bite was alive with flavor and sunlight.

As evening came, the sky turned lavender and rose. We walked hand in hand to the edge of the cliff and watched the sun melt into the sea. I could feel my heart bowing in gratitude—for the love beside me, for the sea before me, for the home that sings my name Night fell like a soft curtain. Stars scattered across the sky, and the sound of the sea deepened. We had a simple dinner by candlelight, a vegetarian stew with herbs we picked ourselves, and a slice of pineapple still warm from the sun.

Later, we curled up in the hammock on the veranda. He whispered stories, and I let the night breeze braid its fingers over my bare scalp. I could feel it then—this life is more than a dream. It is a prayer, answered in advance. And as I write this by lamplight, I know this truth: I was always meant for this softness, this love, this sea.

THE BECOMING WHOLE

Letters To The Woman I Am Collection

Because this journey is more than words on a page...it is something you can sip, hold, light, and live.

On the pages ahead, you'll discover a few quiet companions—pieces created to deepen the mood of the book and to honor the rituals of self-care and love.

Becoming Whole Oolong

A slightly oxidized treasure from Anxi County, China. Floral and gentle, with the elegance of green tea and the depth of something ancient. Each sip is an invitation to slow down and savor the moment.

Becoming Whole Candle

Amber and sandalwood in a soft, glowing embrace. Light it as you write, reflect, or dream—its fragrance wrapping your space in warmth and grounded beauty.

Becoming Whole Mug

A smooth white porcelain mug, created for those sacred moments when your tea and your thoughts meet. Every curve is designed to feel right in your hands.

Becoming Whole Card Deck

Forty-six cards of reflection, guidance, and gentle questions. Draw one each morning or in moments of uncertainty and let the wisdom lead you home to yourself.

Becoming Whole Tote Bag

A sturdy, stylish canvas tote designed for carrying your book, journal, or daily essentials. Printed with the Becoming Whole design, it's a piece of the journey you can take anywhere.

Becoming Whole T-Shirt

Soft cotton, beautifully cut, and emblazoned with the Becoming Whole message. Wear it as a reminder that you are sacred, you are whole.

Becoming Whole: Companion Journal

A guided journey with letters, reflections, and the woman you are becoming. This journal is your companion, a sacred space for reflection. Within these pages, you will be invited to pause, breathe, and listen to your own voice. Each section offers words to inspire, prompts to guide you, and space to write the story of your wholeness.

Here is a sneak peek at the Chapters:

Chapter 1 – I Am Sacred

Chapter 2 – I Am My Own Rescue

Chapter 3 – Choosing Joy

Chapter 4 – Gratitude as Medicine

Chapter 5 – I am Enough

Chapter 6 – Releasing What No Longer Serves

Chapter 7 – Trusting My Bounce Back

Chapter 8 – The Power of Boundaries

Chapter 9 – Listening to My Inner Voice

Chapter 10 – Loving Myself Fully

Chapter 11 – Walking Through Fear

Chapter 12 – Honoring My Body

Chapter 13 – Healing Old Wounds

Chapter 14 – Living with Intention

Chapter 15 – Becoming Whole

Closing Ceremony

Beloved, you have walked through letters, questions, and your own becoming. May these pages remind you that healing is possible, that joy is within reach, and that you are your own beautiful rescue. Close this journal not as an ending, but as a continuation of your story—still unfolding, still becoming.

Acknowledgements

With all my love, Becoming a woman is no solitary act, it is a becoming shaped by love, held by memory, refined in fire, and softened by the laughter of those who dare to stand beside you, who see you, who whisper, "Keep going."

To Yvonne Ruddock and Tanya Ryan, you are the Keepers of the Secrets, the quiet holders of truth, of lineage, of medicine women's grace. Thank you for walking with me through this sacred unfolding. For guarding the mysteries with tenderness and letting me write them down in my own trembling way. You are sacred to this work.

To all the women who have walked with me, cried with me, prayed over me, called me by name, and reminded me I was not too much and never not enough— this book is for you.

To my ancestors—thank you for the dreams. To the ones I've loved and the ones who broke me open— you, too, made me whole.

And to the Divine—the One who sees, who heals, who calls forth the woman in me, again and again. God hold each of you in the palm of His hands and be really good to you, the way you've been really good to me.

With all my love,

Lorna

Contact Author

For speaking engagements, book signings or wellness coaching inquiries please contact:

Lorna Owens
Founder
Desert Sage Lifestyle Wellness
Website: www.desert-sage.co

Store Location
101 Artisan Alley
DeLand, Florida 32720

Follow us on Instagram: @desertsagelifestyle

Lorna Owens Esq
305-505-5493
www.desert-sage.co
www.footprints-foundation.org

www.ingramcontent.com/pod-product-compliance
Lightning Source LLC
Chambersburg PA
CBHW032030290426
44110CB00012B/747